PLAYS BY

EDWARD ALBEE

(DATES OF COMPOSITION)

THE LADY
FROM
DUBUQUE

EDWARD ALBEE

THE LADY FROM DUBUQUE

A PLAY

NEW YORK 1980

ATHENEUM

Copyright © 1977, 1980 by Edward Albee
All rights reserved
Published simultaneously in Canada by McClelland and Stewart Ltd.
Library of Congress catalog card number 78–3192
ISBN 0–689–10925–3
Manufactured by American Book–Stratford Press, Saddle Brook, New Jersey
Designed by Harry Ford
First Edition

FOR

STEPHANI HUNZINGER

—FROM THE BEGINNING

FIRST PERFORMANCE

January 31, 1980, The Morosco Theater, New York City

Lucinda   CELIA WESTON   *Edgar*   DAVID LEARY

Sam   TONY MUSANTE   *Carol*   MAUREEN ANDERMAN

Jo   FRANCES CONROY   *Oscar*   EARLE HYMAN

Fred   BAXTER HARRIS   *Elizabeth*   IRENE WORTH

Directed by ALAN SCHNEIDER

Setting   ROUBEN TER-ARUTUNIAN

Costumes   JOHN FALABELLA

Lighting   RICHARD NELSON

Stage Manager   JULIA GILLETT

CHARACTERS

The characters in order of speaking are:

SAM   *a good-looking, thinnish man; 40*

JO   *a frail, lovely, dark-haired girl; early 30's*

FRED   *a blond ex-athlete going to fat; 40*

LUCINDA   *your average blonde housewife; 35*

EDGAR   *balding perhaps; average; 40*

CAROL   *brunette; ripe; 30*

OSCAR   *an elegant, thin black man; 50 or so*

ELIZABETH   *a stylish, elegant, handsome woman; splendid for whatever her age.*

SET

A living room with stairs to the second floor and a balcony; a bay window; an all-purpose entrance hall.

I see the environment as uncluttered, perhaps with a Bauhaus feeling. No decorator has been at work; what we see is the taste of the occupants. I think the predominant color should be light grey.

PERFORMANCE NOTE

With some regularity throughout this play the characters address the audience—usually in brief asides, but occasionally at greater length. This is done without self-consciousness, quite openly, and without interrupting the flow of the play. In other words, the characters are aware of the presence of the audience, and since the audience has always been there, the characters are not upset by it, even though there are times they wish it would go away.

It is of utmost importance that the actors make it clear that it is not they, but the characters, who are aware of the presence of the audience.

Speeches to the audience (asides, etc.) are clearly marked, as is their termination.

THE LADY
FROM
DUBUQUE

ACT I

SAM, JO, FRED, CAROL, EDGAR, *and* LUCINDA *Onstage.*
EDGAR *Center, his back to the audience;* FRED *at the
bar;* SAM *at the window seat; the* OTHERS *seated or
sprawled. It is midnight;* THEY *are tired and* THEY
have been drinking a little.
The GROUP *applauds* EDGAR *as the curtain rises;* HE
bows to them, exaggerated, mocking. THEY *are playing Twenty Questions, and* EDGAR *has finished his
turn.*

LUCINDA
Good for Edgar! Good for you, Edgar!

SAM
(*Rises, moves Center, as* EDGAR *moves to sit*)
O.K., now; my turn.
(*As the* OTHERS *mumble to each other*)
All right, now; silence! It's my turn! Who am I?

JO
Well, if you don't know who you are, I don't see . . .

FRED
Who's talking?

SAM
C'mon, Fred!

FRED

Who's *talking!?*

EDGAR

O.K., give the man some silence.

JO

The man asked for silence; give it to him.

SAM

From the wives, too?

JO (*Deep voice*)

From the wives, too.

FRED

Who's *talking?*

LUCINDA

You are, for one, Fred.

CAROL

Leave Fred alone.

SAM

From the wives? Please? The girl friends and the wives?

JO

The man asked for silence; give it to him; he doesn't know who he is.

FRED (*Clapping*)

O.K.! O.K.! Let's have a little silence for the man.

SAM

Come on, gang; you've all had a turn, and now it's mine.

FRED

Carol didn't have a turn. Why is it your turn?

SAM

Carol didn't *want* a turn. Besides, it's my house, and you're drinking my liquor, and it's my turn.

FRED (*Shrugs; sits*)

You can't argue with logic.

EDGAR (*To create order*)

O.K. one more time; Sam's turn; Sam goes.

LUCINDA

Remember! Edgar's winning! You all took twelve to get Edgar.

FRED (*Bored*)

Good old Edgar.

EDGAR
(*Hand in champ pose, but weary*)

Yea for me.

SAM

Let me have silence; *please!* Who *am* I?

JO

The man asked for silence; give it to him. Poor man: he doesn't know who he is.

LUCINDA

Let there be silence!

(*There is silence*)

SAM

Well; at last! Thank you! Twenty questions . . . who *am* I?

JO

(*Leans forward; to the audience*)
Don't you just hate party games? Don't you just hate them?
(*Turns her attention back*)

SAM

(*To* JO, *commenting on her involving the audience*)
Come on! Don't do that!
(*To the* OTHERS)
Twenty questions! Who *am* I?

FRED (*Bored*)
Your name is *Sam;* this is your *house* . . .

CAROL

Stop it, Fred; I don't want any help.

FRED

I'm not giving you any!

CAROL

So *you* say.

FRED

Jesus!

SAM

Who am I! Come on! Who am I!?

JO (*Rote*)

Your name is Sam; this is your house; they're drinking your
liquor . . .

SAM

Awwww, Jo . . .

JO

Your name is Sam, and this is your house, and I am your wife,
and I am dying . . .

SAM (*Private*)

Don't, Jo.
                    (*To the* OTHERS)
Come on, gang. Who am I?

EDGAR (*Sighs*)

O.K. one more time

LUCINDA

Let's play!

JO (*Shrugs*)

O.K. let's play.
                    (*To the audience*)
What can you do? He's a nice man.
                    (*Her attention back to the* OTHERS)

EDGAR

Are you a man?

SAM

No.

JO

Coulda fooled *me*.

CAROL (*To* FRED)

Then he's a woman.

FRED

Of course he's a woman! What the fuck do you think he is!?

CAROL (*Getting angry*)

He could be a dog, or a horse, or something!

FRED

A horse!? What do you mean, a horse? Nobody's ever been a horse! You're always embarrassing me!

CAROL

I'm trying to learn the game! You want me to fit in, don't you? Well? Besides, what's embarrassing about a horse?

JO
(*As if the question were to be answered*)
What's embarrassing about a horse? Well, lets see . . .
(*To the audience*)
They're certainly no brighter than you'd want them to be.

SAM

Aw, come on! Hunh? Jo? Please?
(JO *shrugs, turns her attention back in*)

EDGAR (*Bored*)

Play the game; play the game.

CAROL
(*To* SAM, *very unsure of herself*)
You a horse, or something?

SAM (*Smiles*)

Nope; nothing like that.

JO (*To the* GUESTS)

And . . . they're said to bear grudges, but with their tiny brains, I wonder.

LUCINDA (*An announcement*)

Neither a man nor a horse. That's two.

CAROL (*To* FRED; *not pleasant*)

So he's a woman, hunh?

FRED

Ask him!

CAROL

What!? Ask him if he's a woman? I just asked him if he was a horse.

FRED (*Enjoying it finally*)

Yeah; ask him; ask him if he's a woman.

CAROL (*Tiny pause*)

You a woman?

SAM (*Smiles*)

No, I'm not a woman; that's three.

CAROL
(*To* FRED: *enraged with embarrassment*)

You see!?

FRED

Whadda you mean you're not a woman!? You're not a man, you gotta be a woman! What are you: one of those sex changes, or something?

SAM (*Laughs*)
No, I am not one of *those*. That's four down.

EDGAR
Hey, hey, wait! Are you more than one person?

SAM (*Pleased*)
Right!

FRED
Ah, for Christ's . . .

EDGAR
How many people are you? You two people?

SAM
Right; two people; that's six questions.

EDGAR
He's two people, gang. Uh . . . men?

SAM
Right.

LUCINDA
Living!

SAM
Wrong; that's eight.

EDGAR
O.K. Two dead people; both men.

FRED
Probably a couple of queers! Famous queers!

JO

You *would* think of that, Fred.

EDGAR

O.K. Let's see . . . Marx and Engels.

LUCINDA (*A loud whisper*)

Were they queer?

EDGAR

Of course not!

CAROL (*To* FRED)

Marx and who?

FRED

Engels! Marx and Engels!

JO (*To* CAROL; *helpful*)

The Kaufman and Hart of their day.

SAM (*Rueful laugh*)

Oh ho, you just wait!

LUCINDA (*Bright*)

Gilbert and Sullivan, Rimbaud and Verlaine . . .

CAROL (*General*)

Who *are* these people!?

JO

They're foreign, Carol.

SAM

That makes eleven.

JO

They're not foreign?

SAM

No! They're not who she said!

FRED

Lum and Abner, Abbott and Costello, Sacco and Vanzetti, uh . . .

SAM

Nope, nope, nope; fourteen.

EDGAR

Hey, you're not playing it right, guessing wild like that. You gotta be scientific.

JO

Old people, Sam? Very old people?
                    (*To the audience*)
I know who it is.
                    (*Her attention back to the* GROUP)

CAROL

They're dead!

FRED
          (*Trying to remain pleasant*)
She means a long time ago, Carol.

CAROL (*Not convinced*)

Oh.

SAM (*Still enthusiastic*)
Yes, old people; long time ago; long, long time ago.

JO

Were they brothers, Sam?
                    (*To the audience*)
I know who it *is*.
                (*Her attention back to the* GROUP)

SAM

Were they . . . ?
                (HE *realizes* JO *knows the answer*)
Aw, that's not fair, Jo.

LUCINDA (*Happy*)

What's not fair!?

EDGAR (*Brows knitted*)

Yeah. What's not fair?

SAM

Jo knows who it is; that's not fair.

FRED (*The edge of anger*)

What do you mean it's not fair!? It's a game, isn't it? She
knows, she knows.

SAM

Wives shouldn't be allowed to play.

FRED (*Stern*)

Wives play; girl friends play; husbands play; everybody plays.
Who the fuck is it, Jo?

JO (*Smiles*)

Brothers, Sam? A long time ago? And these brothers, by the
faintest of possibilities did they happen to be suckled by a
wolf, and did they happen to found the city of Rome?

SAM (*Real down*)
Yes, yes. Fifteen, sixteen, something; I win.

LUCINDA
Oh, *what's* their name!? Remus and something.

EDGAR (*Overly clear*)
Romulus and Remus.

CAROL (*To* FRED)
I don't *know* any of these people!

JO
Don't worry, Carol; you wouldn't have liked them.

SAM
I win. Big deal. It's no fair—really.
                    (*To the audience*)
Really; it's no fair.
                    (*Back to the* OTHERS)

EDGAR
Sore winner.

SAM
She knew who it was; she could figure it out!
                    (*To the audience*)
She knew all along.
                    (*Back to the* OTHERS)

EDGAR
Awwwwwwwww!

CAROL (*To* JO)
How'd you know?

JO

Weeeellll . . .

SAM

Aw, come on, Jo!

JO (*To quiet* SAM)
No, I think it's nice, shows we . . . I think it's nice.
(*To the* OTHERS)
Sam and I were in bed a couple of nights ago—talking and
sort of lying around—and he was stroking me—which is about
it, now; hey, gang?

EDGAR (*Profound sadness*)

Aw, Jo.

JO
(*To the audience; a little rueful herself*)
Death's door, and all. *And* . . . he had one of my breasts,
and he was sort of bouncing it around a little bit . . .

FRED (To SAM)

You debbil!

JO (*Still to the audience*)
. . . and he started nibbling, and then he started suck-
ing . . .
(To SAM)
. . . which breast was it, Sam?

SAM
(*Embarrassed, therefore cold*)
I don't recall: I was occupied.
(*Refers to the audience*)
For God's sake, Jo!

JO (*To* SAM; *kind*)

It's all right.

(*To the audience*)

You don't mind if I talk about my breasts, do you? Humor the lady a little?

(*To* SAM)

They don't mind.

(*To the* GUESTS)

Which breast *was* it—left, I think. And . . . he said—all of a sudden—he said he was Romulus, and I was the she-wolf, and I asked where his brother Remus was, and he told me not to be greedy . . .

SAM

O.K.! Big deal!

(*A mocking chorus of* "Awwwww, poor SAM; Aw, what's the matter, Sam?; he's embarrassed!" *etc.*)

O.K.! O.K.!

LUCINDA

("*Isn't he too cute for words?*")

Aww . . .

SAM

(*To the audience*)

Now, if you want to know the real and true reason I wouldn't tell her where my brother Remus was . . .

JO

Was that you'd killed him!

(*To the audience*)

He'd built the city—Rome—and he was standing around looking at the fortifications—very proud of himself—and Remus came up, took one look, and said, "Wow! Are those ever lousy fortifications."

(*To* SAM, *now*)
And you killed him. Right on the spot.

LUCINDA
What an unpleasant thing to do!

FRED
(*Leans forward in his chair*)
Oh, *I* don't know; a man's proud of his fortifications.

JO (*A trifle glum*)
Anyhow, that's how it was. Sam wins. I guess it, and Sam wins.

EDGAR (*Not much enthusiasm*)
Anyhow, Sam wins; Sam's the champ. Game's over; hurray!

SAM
(*Playing Romulus; speculative*)
I was always jealous of Remus; I never knew why.

JO
What was it, did he hog the nipples? How many do wolves *have*, for God's sake.

SAM
Oh, there were enough . . . but he took my favorites.

FRED (*Laughing*)
The four or five you liked the most.

SAM
Something like that.

JO (*Glum*)
At least you had a *mother*.

SAM (*Curiously annoyed*)

Oh, come on, Jo!

JO (*Undaunted*)

WELL . . .

SAM

You've got a perfectly good mother!

JO
(*Clearly this is a private argument*)
Yeah? Where is she? Where the hell is she?

SAM (*Spits it out*)

"In the hour of your need?"

JO (*Hard*)
YEAH! IN THE HOUR OF MY GODDAMN NEED!!

EDGAR

Come on, Sam.

JO

Yeah? Big deal!

LUCINDA
(*Bright; maybe just to help*)
I've never met your mother!

JO

Big deal!

LUCINDA (*Offended*)

Well. I'm sorry.

JO (*Ugly mimicking*)

"Well. I'm sorry."

LUCINDA

I mean, I know she lives in New Jersey . . .

JO

Fuck New Jersey!

SAM

Jo . . .

LUCINDA (*Grim*)

With her sister, is it?

JO

Fuck Jo's mother's sister!

SAM

Jo . . .

LUCINDA (*Persisting*)

And you don't see her? Is that it?

EDGAR

Leave it alone, Lu.

LUCINDA (*To* EDGAR; *sotto voce*)

I was merely trying . . .

JO

Fuck merely trying.

SAM

C'mon, Jo.

JO (*Perversely casual*)

O.K. O.K. by *me*.

SAM (*To the audience*)

Jo's mother . . .

JO (*Cheerful*)

Ah, fuck Jo's mother.

SAM (*Still to the audience*)

The lady leaves something to be desired. She's tiny, thin as a rail, blue eyes—darting furtive blue eyes—

JO

Fuck furtive blue eyes.

SAM (*Ibid*)

—pale hair, tinted pink, balding a little; you know; the way women do, when they do. We don't see her much. We don't like her; I don't like her.

LUCINDA

Still; a mother is a mother!

FRED

Jesus!

EDGAR

You just can't leave well enough alone, can you?

JO

"A mother is a mother." I like that!

SAM (*To the others*)

Anyhow, game is over; *I* win: suckled by a wolf, fratricidal but victorious.

E D G A R (*Claps his hands*)
Game's over, kids; game's over.

J O (*Sarcastically enthusiastic*)
Yes, and wasn't it boring? Wasn't it all . . . empty, ulti-
mately? Didn't we waste our time?
(*To the audience; without emotion*)
Especially if you're dying, as I am.

S A M (*So sad and weary*)
Come on, Jo. Please?

J O
(*Shrugs; to* SAM, *and generally to the* GUESTS)
I merely wondered; it doesn't matter; I thought I'd ask; for-
get I said it.

S A M
Please, Jo?

F R E D
(*Rises, empty glass in hand; moves toward the bar*)
Boring? I don't know. I thought it was like every other night
around here; I thought it was fine.

S A M (*To* JO)
I mean, are you tired?

J O (*Waves* SAM *off; to* FRED)
Is this the beginning of your hostility, Fred, or are you still
pretending to be pleasant? I can never quite catch the mo-
ment when you turn.
(*To the audience*)
Fred turns.

(Snaps her fingers)

Just like that.

(Back to the GROUP *now)*

CAROL *(Generally)*

What did Fred do?

(To the audience)

What did Fred do?

(Back to the GROUP *now)*

FRED

(Ponders, with a small smile)

I'm still pretending to be pleasant, I think. Get anyone a
drink?

CAROL *(To no one in particular)*

Leave Fred alone; he's bad enough when he's awful.

FRED

I don't think I understand that, Carol. Who can I make a
drink?

JO

(Holding her empty glass out)

Me.

SAM *(Concerned)*

You all . . . you O.K.?

JO *(Bravura)*

Sure.

FRED

(Moves to JO, *takes her glass)*

A little night crap?

JO

A little what? A little night crap? Fred, you aren't vulgar,
you're just plain dirt common.

FRED

You be careful now; I'm still pretending to be pleasant, but
these social events are wearing on a man.

JO

Mmmmmmm; what a pity they're compulsory.

SAM (*Guardedly pleased*)

Hey, come on; I'll think you two like each other.

FRED (*Muses*)

Ooooh, I wouldn't worry, Sam; I like Jo a lot bettern'n Jo
likes me.
(*To* JO; *twang*)
But ah'll make it up to ya, honey; you just see.
(*Normal tone again*)
Lucinda? Is Edgar having another drink?
(JO *laughs*)

LUCINDA

Well, ask *him*. Who do you think I *am*?

FRED

Carol? Edgar, what about it? Lucinda says ask *you*.

CAROL

None for me; it's hard enough to follow as it is.

EDGAR

Well . . . what does everyone think?

SAM

About what?

EDGAR

About having a *drink*. Should I have *another?*

SAM (*A tiny pause*)

Most of us don't care, Edgar.

EDGAR (*Curiously hurt*)

Oh. I see.

SAM (*Mildly patronizing*)

I mean, it's the sort of thing a man's just got to decide for himself.

FRED (*A drawl*)

Sam isn't being unfriendly, Edgar, just laying it on the line, as they say.

LUCINDA

You leave Edgar alone.

EDGAR (*Grim*)

Gee, am I glad I asked.

SAM
(*Overly serious and solicitous*)

I think you ought to do what you want to, Edgar.

JO (*A toast*)

Drink 'til you puke!

LUCINDA (*Nervous distaste*)

Jo! That's not *like* you!

JO

I wasn't *talking* about *me*; I was talking about Edgar. If I were Edgar, I would drink 'til I puked.

(*Small smile*)

No offense.

LUCINDA
(*An hysterical little laugh*)

Well! And none taken!

FRED
(*Friendly; an arm around* EDGAR)

I'd think twice about having another drink if I were you, Edgar. My God, all the things that could happen? They coulda put poison in the ice cubes; it's three blocks home . . . in the *dark*; the sky might fall? And . . . if Doomsday comes, mushroom Doomsday . . .

EDGAR
(*Quiet and as dignified as the situation allows*)

I think I will have a drink, Fred; I just think I will.

(HE *goes to the bar, pushing* FRED *aside*)

SAM (*Laughs, nicely*)

Oh, Edgar! Poor, sweet Edgar!

JO (*Shy little girl imitation*)

The sky might fall? And Doomsday come?

(*A long, hollow sound*)

Doooooooooooomsday!

EDGAR (*A little put off*)

Don't you worry about me, Sam; I'm all right.

SAM
(*Looking at the bar; a small pause*)
Oh. Well. Well, in that case I'll get some more soda; we're
out of soda.
(HE *begins to exit*)

FRED (*As* SAM *exits; broad*)
You're a good man, Sam!

JO
Doooooooomsday!
(*To the audience*)
Doomsday. It follows Thursday . . . if you're lucky.

EDGAR
You all right, Jo?

FRED (*Sitting, heavily*)
Good man, Sam. You have a good husband, Jo.

JO
(*Back to the* OTHERS, *now; to* FRED; *deep voice*)
Thanks, Fred.
(*To* EDGAR; *nice*)
Sure thing, Edgar; I'm O.K.

FRED
No, I mean it; he's O.K.

LUCINDA (*Cheerful*)
Everybody likes Sam. Well, *I* like Sam, too.

FRED (*None too pleasant*)
Hey, that's swell, Lucinda.

(*To the audience*)
We *do* like Sam; Sam's really O.K. We like Sam a lot.

E D G A R (*To the audience*)
Oh, we do; we *like* Sam.

J O
God! What are you planning to do—*knife* him, or something?
(FRED *and* EDGAR *turn their attention back to* JO)

F R E D (*Angry*)
We *like* him, for Christ's sake!

E D G A R
Come on, Jo!

J O
We *all* like Sam! Great! Big deal!
(*Ruminative*)
We all like Sam, and that should make it Samsday. Samsday
precedeth Doomsday: Samsday, Thurmsday, Doomsday. Isn't
that how it goes, Fred?

F R E D (*Casual*)
I don't give a shit, Jo, *how* it goes; just *stop* it!

J O
O.K.

F R E D
All I care about right now is my drink.

J O (*A mock aside, to* CAROL)
Fred really doesn't deserve Sam's friendship; Sam's too good
for Fred; Sam knows it, but . . . well, you know.

FRED (*Much too casual*)

Knock it off, Jo.

JO (*To the audience*)

Sam's a real egalitarian; Sam pretends to like everyone equally. (*Looks to* FRED *for his reaction;* HE *gives her the finger*)

CAROL (*Looking at her nails*)

Sounds sort of indiscriminate to me.

JO

(*As* FRED *chuckles; briefly taken aback; to* CAROL)

Well, yes, it *is* that. But Sam is a man of facets. Who *are* you, Carol?

CAROL (*Stretches*)

Ooooooh, I'm a lady of parts; I got facets, too, you know.

FRED

She's a lady of parts.

CAROL

By which I mean I'm not all bimbo; I'm not your dumb brunette for nothing. I'm gonna go pee.

FRED

You, uh . . . you know where it is?

CAROL

(*Hand on hip; feigns puzzling it out*)

Well, let's see; it's either outdoors or inside, and since this is the sort of neighborhood's probably got zoning regulations I bet I'll find it somewhere here on the ground floor.

FRED (*Sorry HE brought it up*)

O.K. O.K.

CAROL (*Relentless*)

And if I don't find it, I'll just squat on the rug. O.K.? O.K.,
lover?

FRED

O.K.! O.K.!

CAROL
(*To the audience, as* SHE *exits*)

God! These people!

JO (*Looks after* CAROL)

She's not bad; she's got a good mouth.

FRED

Carol's gonna marry me one day.

JO
(*In reaction to* FRED's *remark*)

Not a very good brain, maybe . . .

FRED

I'm a three-time winner; might as well make it four.

EDGAR

Have you asked her?

FRED

Hm?

EDGAR

Have you asked her to marry you!?

FRED

Have I *asked* her!? I ask her every night before we go to sleep; I ask her when we get up; I ask her when I'm in the saddle . . .

LUCINDA (*Smiles at the memory*)

I made Edgar propose to me three times.

JO (*After a slight pause*)

You take big chances, girl.

FRED (*Intensely serious*)

Edgar, if I'd known that, I sure woulda been nicer to you all these years. I'll make it up to you, fella!

JO (*Imitating*)

I'll make it up to you, fella! Big pal; big fella!

EDGAR (*Weary*)

Lay off, Jo.

FRED

No, no, it's all right.

(*Histrionic*)

Where else can you come in this cold world, week after week, as regular as patchwork, and be guaranteed ridicule and contempt? Where else, I ask you, in this cold world?

(*To the audience*)

There is nowhere else, in this cold world, where you can come, week after—

JO (*Level*)

Oh, there must be lots of other places, Fred. *You* have friends; this can't be the only place.

EDGAR

Is the pain bad, Jo?

JO (*Offhand*)

Pretty bad.

LUCINDA (*A little dreamy*)

We love you, Fred; we all love each other.

JO

Speak for yourself, Lu.

FRED (*Not to the audience*)

Name one; name one other place; name one other place where I can come and be *sure* of it, where I can *count* on it.

EDGAR (*Bland*)

Well, you could come to *our* place, Fred; we got as much ridicule and contempt as the next house.

LUCINDA
(*Snapped out of her revery*)

We have not!

(*To the audience*)

That is not true!

(*To* EDGAR)

Really, Edgar!

EDGAR (*Dogmatic*)

Well, we *should*. If you are managing the house as you're supposed to, *if* you are keeping the larder full, then we should have just as much ridicule and contempt as the next . . .

FRED (*Ruminative*)

I used to have *lots* of it—*closets* full; open a cupboard, and
the ridicule and contempt'd just . . . fall out all over the
place! I don't know what happened.

JO (*Soothing*)

Well, maybe when you and Carol get married everything'll
get back to normal.

FRED (*Overly concerned*)

Gee; I sure hope so.
   (A *rumpus Offstage; the sound of* CAROL *and* SAM
   arguing. CAROL *catapults Onstage, followed by* SAM
   with his soda bottles)

CAROL (*At* SAM)

Just keep your fucking hands off me, that's all!!

SAM

Will you shut up!? Will you just—

CAROL

Goddamn creep! Goddamn son of a bitch! Jesus, you can't
even go take a leak around here!

SAM

I said, shut up about it!

CAROL

Just keep your fucking hands off me!

FRED
(*Realizing what is happening*)

Hey hey hey hey!

CAROL (*To* JO; *quivering*)

You better put locks on your bathroom doors, lady, or hand-
cuffs on this one!

FRED

Hey! What the hell *is* this!?

LUCINDA (*Thrilled*)

What's going on!? What's going on!?

EDGAR

What *is* this?

SAM
(*Making weapons out of the soda bottles*)
Will you just shut up about it!?

CAROL

You dirty, dirty old man!

FRED
(*Getting to his feet; belligerent*)
O.K. now, just what the fuck's going—

CAROL
(*A sudden imitation of a violated maiden; falsetto*)
Fred? Would you take me home, please? I've been vastly in-
sulted!

FRED (*Ready for battle now*)
You're fuckin-A right I will! Jesus Christ, Sam!
(*But* CAROL *and* SAM *have dissolved into laughter,
are hanging on to each other for support*)

SAM

Oh, boy; oh, boy!

CAROL

Christ! Oh, Jesus!

EDGAR

Hey, what *is* this? Another game?

CAROL

Oh, Jesus! Oh, sweet Jesus!

SAM

Oh, hey! Wow!

FRED

What the fuck's going on!?

SAM (*Hugging* CAROL)

Oh, boy! Hey, we ought to work up an act!

CAROL

Oh, God, that was fun!
                    (SHE *sees that* FRED *is not amused*)
Fred! Hey, Fred!
                    (SHE *goes to him, hugs him*)
Hey, Fred!

FRED (HE *flings her arm away*)

It's all *right!* Just . . . it's all right. Let go of me!

LUCINDA (*Rather sour*)

That was a *joke.* Is that it?
                    (*To the audience*)
Is that what everybody's laughing about? That it was a joke?

SAM
(*Very pleased with himself*)
Yes, Lu; that was a joke.

LUCINDA
(*Ugly little smile; to* SAM)
I just want to keep up. I don't want to fall behind all you
bright types.

EDGAR (*Hugs her*)
Luuuuuuuuuu!

FRED
(*Trying to recover his dignity*)
That was very funny; you got a big rise out of me, and it was
very funny;
(*Indicates the audience*)
everybody had a good laugh.

SAM
Awwwww, Fred!

JO (*Challenging*)
Including you, Fred?

FRED (*Bluff*)
Sure! Sure!
(*The* OTHERS *are silent*)
No! To be truthful, *no*.

CAROL (*Sincere*)
Aw, Fred.

FRED
No! I rose to the bait, I took it, and I was hauled in. I was
humiliated!

EDGAR

No! You weren't!

CAROL

Awwww, Fred!

SAM

You just showed you cared, Fred.

FRED (*Heavily sarcastic*)

Yeah? Is that it?

CAROL

Yeah! That's it!

FRED (*Shrugs*)

O.K. that's it. You saw me with all my clothes off.

JO (*A half-smile*)

How come you don't hit somebody, Fred? This isn't like you.

FRED

Yeah; I know.

LUCINDA (*Bright*)

Oh, that's interesting!

EDGAR (*Really fed up*)

Why don't you just shut up, Lu?
    (SHE *glares at him for quite a while;* HE *ignores her*)

FRED (*Ingenuous*)

Maybe I'm getting soft; maybe I like you guys.

SAM

Maybe you're in love.

FRED *(Shrugs)*

Maybe I'm in love.
                    (To the audience)
Maybe I'm in love.

JO *(Into her glass)*

I wouldn't count on it.

SAM

Aw, come on, Jo.

FRED *(To Carol)*

You gonna marry me, Carol?
                    (To the audience)
Carol's gonna marry me one day.

JO

You gonna marry Fred one day, Carol?

CAROL
(Appraises FRED; *to the* OTHERS*)*
I don't know. How many of us end up marrying Fred?

FRED *(To the* GROUP*)*

Three, so far; I'm a three-time winner. You wanna marry me,
Carol? Christ, now I'm asking her in public! Three-time
winner, Carol; you wanna make it four?

CAROL
(Very true, if nose-wrinkling)
I don't *know*.

(*To the audience*)
Really. I don't know.

SAM (*To* JO)
Four of a kind isn't bad.

J O (*Shrugs*)
Beats a full house.

EDGAR
You gonna marry Fred, Carol?

C A R O L (*Quite pestered*)
I don't know, I don't know, I don't know! I know it's late
and I got the itch, but beyond that I'm not sure.

FRED
I should drink up?

CAROL
Suit yourself; I've done it solo.

F R E D (*Sighing, rising*)
Maybe we ought to go, host and hostess.

L U C I N D A (*Rises, nudges* EDGAR)
Well, we certainly are. Come on, Edgar.

F R E D (*Sits again*)
Oh, well, then, we'll stay.

SAM
(*To* LUCINDA *and* EDGAR; *only mildly protesting*)
Oh? You . . . taking off?

EDGAR (*Reluctantly rising*)

Apparently.

JO (*Moody; to the audience*)

Hardly anyone stays up late anymore. Why do you think that is?

LUCINDA (*To JO; a schoolmarm*)

It's because we all get tired earlier than we used to.

JO

(*Still to the audience; sags her shoulders; great, mock defeat*)

Oh, God! Do you think it's that!?

EDGAR

Thank you, Sam—especially for the games, all of 'em.
(*To JO; a concerned tone; light, though*)
You take it easy, Jo.

JO (*To EDGAR; toasts him*)

Alley-oop!

EDGAR

(*An arm around SAM's shoulder now*)
Night, you two; you suffer fools so gladly; it's a gift.

JO (*Salutes EDGAR*)

Help yourself, if there's any left.

EDGAR

Remember the alimony, Fred; remember the itch, but remember the alimony.

(FRED *waves*)

LUCINDA (*Generally*)
Good night, now; good night.
(*No one reacts.*
To the audience; quite peeved)
No one says good night to me, you may have noticed.

JO
Nobody says good night to you? Not even Edgar?

LUCINDA (*To* JO)
Well, of course *Edgar* says good night to me!

JO (*Deep chest tone*)
Well, then!

LUCINDA (*Sort of hysterical*)
Of course, Edgar more or less *has* to say good night to me!

JO
Still! Count your blessings!

LUCINDA (*Beady-eyed and tough*)
My cup runneth over, hunh?

JO
Right! But watch the rug.

EDGAR
Come on, Lu, let's get you out of here in one piece. Be good
to one another.

JO
Any particular order we should do that in?

EDGAR
Nah; touch one, touch all.

LUCINDA (*Eyes narrowing; to* JO)

Just what did you mean by "count your blessings"? Just what did you mean by that?

EDGAR (*Eyes to heaven*)

Oh, Christ!

SAM

What are you two going to do now, have a fight, or something?

LUCINDA (*Clearly spoiling*)

No, we're not going to have a fight; I merely want to know what Miss Smartypants here means by "count your blessings," that's all.

EDGAR

Oh, Christ!

JO (*Rising to it*)

All I meant *was*—my *dear* Lucinda—that you are lucky . . . that *any*one . . . says good night to you, by which I sus*pect* I meant . . .

SAM

Oh, God.

JO (*Louder*)

By which I sus*pect* I meant you're lucky you've got anybody living in the same *house* with you, much less merely *talk*ing to you.

LUCINDA (*Stiff; cold*)

I see.

JO

Is that *clear?*

LUCINDA (*Nose out of joint*)

I think *so;* thank you very *much.*

JO (*Drawl*)

Ooooooh, you're welcome; my goodness, you're welcome.

EDGAR

Come on, Lu.

SAM (*Quietly cajoling*)

Be *nice,* Jo.

LUCINDA (*Grand, if stern*)

I'm going to forgive you, Jo.

JO (*Deep tone again*)

Thanks, Lu.

SAM

Jo . . .

LUCINDA (*None too kind*)

I'm going to forgive you because I assume the pain is very
bad.

(*A general silence*)

JO (*Sighs, stares at the ceiling*)

Well, nothing compared to the one you give me, Lu.

(*Snarls*)

Get out of here, will you!?

LUCINDA

(*A brave smile; to the audience*)

Jo used to have at me this way when we were at college—
making fun of me all the time.

(*To the* OTHERS, *now*)

It's become a habit; we don't even know we're doing it anymore.

JO (*Pretending consternation*)

Gee, I thought *I* knew.

EDGAR (*Pulls at* LUCINDA)

Come on; get out of here before you're plucked clean.

LUCINDA (*To* FRED *and* CAROL)

She really doesn't know she's doing it.

EDGAR (*Impatient with her*)

O.K.; O.K.!

(*To* SAM *and* JO; *drawled*)

Thank you, you two; it was your nice, average, desperate
evening; we had fun.

SAM

So did we; so did we!

FRED

So did we!

CAROL

Yeah!

JO

(*Still pretending to be puzzled*)

I thought I *knew* I was having at her; I could *swear* I *knew*.

LUCINDA (*Close to tears*)

Come on, Edgar; Jo's "tired."

JO (*Mocking*)

"Jo's tired." Fuck off.

EDGAR (*Gentle*)

Take it easy, Jo. Night, Sam.

SAM
(*Goes to the hall with them*)

Let me come with you.

EDGAR

No, no; come on!

JO

"Let me come with you." "No, no; come on."
(*Calls after, too bouyant*)
Night! Thanks for coming!
(*To* FRED *and* CAROL)
Wanna keep me alive? Wanna cause a remission?

FRED (*Smiles nicely*)

What do I have to do—kill Lucinda?

JO

That'd sure help.
(*To herself, mostly*)
Wouldn't do any good, but it'd sure help.

CAROL (*Trying to help*)

I lost a sister.

JO

What'd you do, leave her in the parking lot, or something?

CAROL (*Tiny pause*)

Skip it.

(*A silence;* SAM *reenters*)

JO

Night? Thanks for coming?

SAM

Is it? *Is* it very bad?

JO (*Transparent*)

What? Is what?

SAM

The pain. Is it very bad?

JO (*A harsh laugh*)

It could be worse . . . they keep telling me.
(*Shrugs*)
Nah; I just don't like her.

SAM (*Gentle correction*)

C'mon; I know you.

JO (*Dismissive*)

Change the record.

SAM

Look, I'm not one to complain . . .

JO

Good! Pull up a drink and sit down; join us.

FRED

Clear a space somewhere; c'mon in; the Scotch and water's
fine.

SAM (*Views the room; sighs*)

I don't know how six people can make such a mess of a perfectly good . . .

JO

Leave it. Let it pile up.
                    (SAM *laughs, shrugs*)

Tired, baby?

SAM

Lots of things. Why do we ask them over, Jo?

JO
                    (*A child giving the correct answer*)

Because they're our friends, tha's why.

SAM

God, you're awful to Lucinda.

FRED (*Feigned surprise*)

Jo? Awful? To Lucinda?

JO (*By way of apology*)

Everybody's awful to Lucinda, except Edgar, maybe, and who knows?

SAM

No; everybody makes *fun* of Lucinda, but you're *awful* to her.

JO (*Languid*)

Well, maybe we ought to even it out more. You want to be awful to her next time? How about you, Fred?

FRED (*Helpful*)

Sure, I'll do it.

SAM (*To* JO)

Be careful; you may need Lucinda one day.

JO (*Laughs*)

Who? Me?

(*Detached*)

Well, I dare say the day will come I'll need you all. Then, of course, the day will come I won't need a soul. And then, of course, the day won't come.

SAM (*Little-boy sad*)

Oh, Jo.

JO (*To the audience, as above*)

That's what they tell us, isn't it—that growing pile of books on how to die? That somewhere along the line you stop needing those you . . . need the most? You loose your ties? God, what do you need then?

(*To* SAM; *some energy*)

Hey! Rub my shoulders.

SAM (*Moves to her; begins*)

Why *do* we have them over, Jo?

JO

Why do we have *anyone* over? Less on the neck when I'm trying to talk, or is that the idea? Why do we have them over? Did I say because we love them?

SAM (*Rubbing her shoulders*)

Nope; you said because they were our friends.

JO (*Offhand*)

Oh. Well, add because we love them, but secretly mean because we need a surface to bounce it all off of . . .

SAM

I'm moving back toward the neck.

JO

I'm almost done. Because! Because it's too much trouble to change it all, and because we probably do love them in spite of everything . . .

SAM (*Examining her neck*)

There's meant to be a pressure point, a nerve right about here on the neck . . .

JO

O.K.! O.K.! If you're going to ask me broody-type questions, don't expect me to be . . .

SAM

Lucinda isn't all that bad.

JO

Yes, she *is*.

FRED

She *is*, Sam.

CAROL

Oh, yes; she really is.

SAM (*To the* THREE *of them*)

She's no worse than Edgar for putting up with it—with *her*.

JO

What she's no worse than is your friend Fred, the floozy-bopper; that one over there.

SAM

What's the matter with Fred?

CAROL *(Eyes narrowing)*

The what?

FRED

What's the matter with me?

JO

You're a pain; that's what's the matter with you.

CAROL
(Assimilating it, with interest)

The floozy-bopper?

SAM

What's Fred ever done to you?

FRED

Yeah. What've I ever done to you?
                    (Wiggles his eyebrows)
'Cept in my mind, maybe?

CAROL

Floozy-bopper?
                    (Grudging admiration)
That's pretty good.

JO *(Swings around to FRED)*

What have you done to me? You have subjected me to three
—count 'em, three!—of what I assume is to be an endless
parade of wives, each of whom is further from the mark than
the previous one.

SAM (*The peacemaker*)

Well, now he's got Carol.

FRED

And Carol's different.

SAM

And, besides, it's his business.

JO

Shut up! I'm being irrational! It is *not* his business; we have to put up with it. Besides, he's a reactionary, Nixon-loving fag baiter; he's . . .

FRED

Nobody's a Nixon-lover; nobody ever *was* a Nixon-lover; nobody even voted for him; ever! Don't you keep up?

JO (*Grudging*)

Well, that's true. Still! I don't like you, Fred, when you get right down to it.

FRED (*No help at all*)

I like *you*.

JO (*Head back; Bernhardt*)

Oh, God! Oh, God! The burdens!
        (*Wriggles free*)
What are you doing? Fiddling with me? God!

SAM (*Mild*)

The lady don't want to be coddled no more?

JO

Coddle me not.

(*Afterthought*)

On the lone prairie.

> (SHE *rises, stretches, begins to move about; suddenly*
> SHE *is bent double with pain;* SHE *falls back on her*
> *footstool, her hands clutching her belly.* SHE *howls;*
> *it is a sound of intense agony and protest at the same*
> *time. It is not very loud, but profound.* SAM *stands*
> *where* HE *is, watches. A silence; then* SHE *howls*
> *again; same nonreaction from* SAM, *though* CAROL
> *covers her ears and leans in toward* FRED, *who cud-*
> *dles her.*
>
> EDGAR *has come back in during this last.* HE *is framed*
> *in the doorway*)

E D G A R (*Into the silence*)

Please?

(*Pause*)

Hello?

S A M (*Great weariness; sighs*)

Hello, Edgar.

F R E D

What did you forget, Edgar? Your youth? Your dignity,
your—

E D G A R (*Cutting* FRED *off*)

Neither; both; take your pick. Jo?

> (HE *walks over to* JO; SHE *looks up at him with*
> *pleading and pain; no sound, though.*
> *Softly*)

Jo, I came back because Lucinda is . . . because Lucinda is
sitting out on the lawn, crying her heart out.

FRED (*Sotto voce*)

On the lawn?

(*Now, and during the rest of* EDGAR's *following speech,* JO *will howl from time to time, not very loud, but intense, as a counterpoint to his remarks*)

EDGAR

(*A dismissing gesture to* FRED; *then*)

We get outside, Jo, and we start across the lawn, and she plops right down and she starts crying, right there. She says she can't take it anymore, Jo, the way you go at her; the way you make such terrible fun of her in front of everybody! She says it was all right until you got sick but now you're sick you mean it in a different way, and it's breaking her heart.

(SHE *howls*)

Don't do that, Jo; I'm trying to *tell* you. Lucinda's down there on the lawn, and she's pulling up tufts of grass and throwing 'em around, and she's got dirt all over her, and I don't think it's any crap: she means it; she's not going to get up from that fucking lawn 'til you say you're sorry. So I think you better get down there and help her—apologize, or what—in spite of your pain, because she's in pain down there, too, and she didn't cause yours.

(*A silence*)

JO (*To the audience*)

Well, I don't suppose there's any answer to that 'cept get up and go down there with her—"sit upon the ground and tell sad stories"?

(*To the* OTHERS *now*)

Tear up a few mutual tufts, hold on to each other, rock, console? I guess I'd better.

SAM

No, Jo!

J O

Edgar's right: Lucinda's in pain.

(JO *rises, clearly still in some pain herself*)

OWWW! And pain is less fun than a few other things. Can
I have a hand?

(SHE *puts her hands out;* SAM *helps her up*)

CAROL

You want your shoes?

J O

Nah, it's bedtime; besides, the grass tickles; I like it. Edgar?
I'll set it right as best I can; no promises; your wife ain't easy;
she can turn a kindly phrase sour in the best of mouths, but
I'll try.

EDGAR (*Sincere*)

Thank you, Jo.

JO (*To* SAM)

Give Edgar a drink; give him some comfort; tell him some
lies.

SAM

(As THEY *move toward the hallway*)

Easy. You're so light.

J O

I weigh nothing; I'm air. Off to the lawn.

FRED

We better go, too. C'mon, toots.

SAM

Be careful, Jo; it may be damp.

CAROL (*Not too enthusiastic*)
O.K.

JO
You mean I may get a cold to go with the rest?

FRED
(*Moving to* JO, *taking her from* SAM)
One strong arm.

JO
What's the matter with the other one?

FRED
Take it easy, lady.

JO (*A laugh*)
What is all this—in case I fall? In case I become dust on the threshold?

FRED
Take her other arm, Carol.

CAROL
She can make it; she's a good girl.

JO (*To* SAM)
I'm a good girl.

SAM
Come back, Jo.

JO
I'm a good girl. Who are you?
(JO *exits, with* FRED *and* CAROL)

SAM (*To the empty hallway*)
You're a good girl; come back.
(EDGAR *stays standing;* SAM *doesn't look at him, but
picks up a few glasses*)

EDGAR (*Finally*)
Do you want to talk?

SAM
Nope.

EDGAR
You want to make me a drink?

SAM
Nope.

EDGAR
Uh . . . you want to give me some comfort? You want to
tell me some lies?

SAM (*Almost laughing*)
Oh . . . go make your own drink.

EDGAR
(*An imitation: what? a girl?*)
Gee, I thought you'd never ask.

SAM (*Sitting*)
You *want* some comfort? You *want* some lies?

EDGAR (*Looking*)
I want some bourbon.

SAM

Right in front of you. O.K., let's see: *you're* looking well; *Lucinda's* looking well; *Fred's* looking well; *Carol's* looking well . . .

EDGAR
(*Concentrating on his drink*)
Very funny.

SAM

Jo's looking well; *I'm* looking well . . .

EDGAR (*Abrupt, but not loud*)
Can't you control her? Even a little? You let Jo just run wild these days, these nights?

SAM (*Looks away; sighs*)
Yeah, I pretty much let her do what she wants to do.

EDGAR (*Cool*)
You figure that's best?

SAM (*Unintimidated*)
I figure that's best.

EDGAR (*Pause; rather arch*)
Well, I suppose that's the way it ought to be. I mean, I suppose you should know.

SAM (*Closing the subject*)
I suppose I should know.

EDGAR (*Muted*)
I suppose you should.

(*Pause;* he *slams his drink down*)
JESUS CHRIST, WHAT KIND OF A HOUSE DO YOU
RUN AROUND HERE!?

s a m · (*Too calm, if anything*)

Hm? Pardon me?

e d g a r
YOUR FUCKING GUESTS END UP CRYING!?

s a m (*Still calm*)
They love us: they cry. Look to your own house, buddy.

e d g a r
(*Intense, but less loud than before*)
People don't cry at *our* house! People don't come over and
visit *us* and go away sobbing!

s a m (*Harsh*)
No! They go away laughing! Behind your back, of course, but
laughing!

e d g a r (*Clearly an old subject*)
Oh, Christ, not that again, hunh!? I am not you; Lucinda is
not Jo; black is not white, and when the fuck are you going to
get it all straight?

s a m
(*Shakes his head; mock consternation*)
I keep *trying;* I keep *trying.*

e d g a r
I *know* you don't like the way I run my marriage . . .

SAM

I didn't know you ran it.

EDGAR

What? I know you don't even *like* Lucinda, for that matter; *any* of you!

SAM (*Mock shock*)

Oh! How did you ever figure that out!? We've kept it so . . . so . . .

EDGAR (*Serene; even superior*)

But I don't *care*.

SAM

Oh, that's clear.

EDGAR

I decided a long time ago that the fact I love Lucinda gives her all the virtue she needs—if there's any lack to begin with. It's a common enough thing; we all do it; I just admit it.

SAM (*Almost a sneer*)

Well, I dare say you'd have to.

EDGAR (*Furious*)

You're no different!

SAM (*Cool*)

Edgar, you're my only friend whose every virtue embarrasses me. You're the only man I know does something good and I want to hit him.

EDGAR (*So reasonable*)

Well, I guess you *need* me, Sam.

SAM

I'm not into M and S.

EDGAR

S and M.

SAM

What?

EDGAR (*Turning a little nasty*)

Yeah, I guess you need me. I mean, shit!, what's a martyr for 'less there's someone 'round the corner to do him in? Fred'd never turn on me: he's too straightforward; Carol hasn't been around long enough to learn the game.

SAM

Any game.

EDGAR

What? Jo has her own problems, and so that just leaves you, ol' buddy. I don't need to take my shirt off, do I? You got a whip goes right through cloth, don't you? You say you're not into it?

SAM (*Smiles; to the audience*)

It's the self-indulgence of these martyrs gets me most.

EDGAR (*Smiles; to* SAM)

Is it? Does it? Glad you got it pinpointed.
(*Pause; gentle*)

Can I help?

SAM
(*To* EDGAR; *pause; shakes his head*)

Nobody can help.

EDGAR

Can *any* of us help?

SAM

Nobody can help.

EDGAR (*Acknowledgment*)

Not even the village martyr.

SAM

Move *over*.

EDGAR (*As above*)

Yeah; sure thing.

SAM
(*Looks up; tears, but no outburst*)

It's a death house I'm keeping here, old friend . . . to answer your question.

EDGAR (*A silence*)

I know; and nobody can help.

SAM

No; nobody.

EDGAR (*Helpless shrug*)

Right!
(*Pause*)

I'll go see how they're doing.

SAM

You do that.

EDGAR (*By the hallway*)

I'll even put the divots back. How's that for friendship?
Hunh?

SAM

Pretty good. Not bad.
  (EDGAR *moves to exit, but stops, listens as* SAM *begins.*
  To the audience/to himself/to anyone)
Each day, each night, each moment, she becomes less and
less. My arms go around . . . bone? She . . . diminishes.
She moves away from me in ways I . . . The thing we must
do about loss is, hold on to the object we're losing. There's
time later for . . . ourselves. Hold on! . . . but, to what?
To bone? To air? To dust?
  (JO *enters as* SAM *begins to weep.* HE *lets his weeping*
  develop, slowly, softly, toward a full expression of
  misery. His shoulders shake; HE *sobs;* HE *lets it spend*
  naturally. As HE *weeps,* JO *replaces* EDGAR *in the*
  archway, EDGAR *exiting.* JO *leans against the hall, ob-*
  serving SAM. HE *becomes aware of her presence;* SHE
  becomes aware of this. HE *finishes his weeping not-*
  withstanding)

JO
  (*When* HE *is about done; seemingly offhand*)
Don't cry; don't cry.

SAM

You cry.

JO
  (*Begins to move about the room*)
Ah. Well.

(*Afterthought*)

Women cry.

SAM

Men cry.

JO (*A smile; apologetic*)

Yes, but if *you* cry, I will, *too*, and haven't I enough? I mean,
if I started crying for myself, what would hold me together?
(SHE *goes to him; strokes his head*)
Help me not to cry? Please?
(HE *buries his head in her crotch, his hands on her
buttocks;* HE *shakes his head slowly*)
Now; now; now.

SAM (*Releases her; turns away*)

None of this is easy, you know.

JO (*Small, sardonic smile*)

Your pain's as bad as mine, eh?

SAM

(*Angry at being misunderstood*)
I didn't *say* that!

JO (SHE *too, angry*)

I didn't *say* you said that!

SAM

Of *course* it's not as bad as yours; it's not even like yours!
What do you take me for?

JO

Husband?

SAM

But I *share* it.

JO (*Strokes his cheek*)

No, you don't, and I'm glad. Yours is almost all in your head
—in your mind, I mean—and mine isn't thank you, ma'am!
(*To the audience*)

God! I wish it *was*—all in my head, in my mind.

SAM (*To* JO, *for her attention*)

You can't measure pain! I'm in pain! I love you!

JO (*To* SAM; *comforting*)

I *know* you are; and I love *you.*
(*To the audience again, with a harsh, abrupt laugh*)

Jesus, that would be funny!—if you could measure pain?

SAM (*Crying again*)

Dear God, stop it! Please?

JO

(*Very gentle; almost lyrical; to* SAM)

All right. See? Stopped.
(*To the audience; shrugs*)

Stopped.
(*A silence.* JO *takes a small pill vial from a pocket*)

SAM (*Sees it*)

How many today? How often are you . . . ?

JO (*Ironic again*)

Popping the old pills? Oh, ten, twelve a day. Guess I better
get myself down to ol' Doc Wheeler for a new prescription
—or a stronger one.

SAM (*Hollow*)

Ten or twelve?

JO (*Laughter in the dark*)

Sure; why not!

SAM

A day?

JO (*Deflated*)

Oh, come on.

SAM

God, Jo.

JO (*A heavy sigh*)

Look, Sambo, you better get used to it. It's not going to get any less and it's not going to get any better. I'm up; I'm moving about; I'm engaged in what they refer to as social intercourse; I don't scream more than seven or eight times a day, on a good day . . .

(SAM *covers his ears, hunches over*)

Don't cover up like that! It's *me* we're talking about!

(SHE *pulls his hands from his ears*)

I say it's *me* we're talking about! Christ, if you can't take it now, what will you be like when I *need* you? *Really* need you!?

(*Afterthought*)

Or something?

SAM (*A truthful answer*)

I don't know.

JO (*Far away*)

No. And I don't know what I'll need.

SAM

No.

(THEY BOTH *seem huddled and sort of lost*)

JO

Well, give it some thought: the day *is* going to come. What did ol' Doc Wheeler say? Don't plan great distances ahead? Like, don't try getting your master's, or anything.

SAM (*Softly*)

You have your master's?

JO

Hm?

SAM

You *have* your master's?

JO

I don't think he knows that; . . . what I think he *meant* was: wind it up; you're winding down, so . . . wind it up.

SAM (*Glum; dogmatic*)

Everything is reversible.

JO (*A vulnerable smile*)

Spontaneous combustion, or whatever they call it?

SAM

Mmm-hmmmm.

JO

But that's the localized ones, or the ones in the blood sometimes . . .

SAM (*Exploding*)
DON'T GIVE ME YOUR FACTS! YOU'RE SO PROUD
OF YOUR FUCKING FACTS!!

JO
(*Calm and steady, to counter his outburst*)
I have a right to know what's going on, 'specially if it's going
on in *me*.

SAM
Let it *go!*

JO
(*Leans in toward him; so dispassionate*)
Some day, when *you're* dying, when *that* day comes, when
the day comes you're *told*, or the day comes you realize
you've known but haven't admitted it, I would dearly love
to be around.

SAM (*Hurt*)
Jo . . .

JO
(*Winces a little: to the audience*)
That isn't *kind, is* it.

SAM
No.

JO (*To* SAM)
No. There are two *theories* on that, you know—on being the
first to go, or not.

SAM
Oh?

JO

Well, there are two theories on *every*thing. One theory is
that dying first is kinder—showing the way, and all, I suppose; none of this "after you" stuff. The other theory is that
"staying on alone," is the gentlemanly thing to do—or the
gentlewomanly, as the case may be.

SAM

Or . . . not doing it at all.

JO

Or . . . not doing it at all.
                         (*Pause*)
Well, yes; *that* has something to be said for it.

SAM (*Absurd and sincere*)

Please? Don't do it at all?

JO

        (*A tiny pause; to the audience; for the sake of not
        letting a silence happen*)
In the *olden* days, in *some* societies, they would do it together—a hubby and wife, when one or the other was
"going"—and in *Egypt*, now, they used to take the servants,
and bury *them* along with . . .

SAM (*Shocked wonder*)

Can't you stop?

JO

        (*Looks at* SAM, *rather surprised to see him; speaks
        to him*)
I say, they used to bury the servants with their masters.
'Course, with the way help is today . . . I'm sorry, Sam;
I'm really sorry.

SAM (*Disgust?*)
What kind of pills are you *taking*, for Christ's sake?

JO
Pain and sleep; pain and sleep. Got any *other* suggestions?
No?
(*Harsh laugh*)
They'll have me on heroin eventually.
(SAM *moves behind her*)
Bet you never knew you were marrying an incipient dopie,
did you; bet you never knew one day you'd have to—
(HE *claps his hand over her mouth, pulls her head
to his body.* SHE *resists momentarily, then turns,
puts her arms around his legs/hips. It is a reversal
of the previous embrace.
A silence*)

SAM (*So gentle*)
We just can't talk about it, it's that simple.

JO (*Finally; subdued*)
There are two theories on that, too. Bet you don't want to
hear them.
(SAM *shakes his head.* JO *rises, moves off a little;*
SAM *stays where* HE *is*)
What was it? You do, or you don't?

SAM
No. No, I don't want to hear them.

JO (*Shrugs*)
Someone's got to listen; someone's got to humor me.

SAM
I listen; I humor you.

JO

Not enough!

SAM (*Sad and weary*)

Jo, you warn me not to humor you, and then you tell me
I'm not . . .

JO (*Doesn't want to hear it*)

I know!

SAM

You tell me to ignore you when you get like this, and then
you yell at me for . . .

JO

I know! I know!! Don't . . . don't . . . just don't . . .
(*Calms down*)
I've got to have it both ways. Don't pay any attention. Pay
attention? Please?

SAM (*Defeated*)

Whatever you want.
(*A silence*)

JO
(*Clearly whistling in the dark*)
Do you think you'll marry again, Sam? Who'll you marry?

SAM

Jo, I . . .

JO

Come on! Play!

SAM

Jo . . .

JO

Come on! Humor me! Who you gonna marry?

SAM (*Hard*)

Carol; naturally.

JO (*Chuckles a little*)

That'd upset old Fred.

SAM

Why? Does old Fred want to marry me?

JO

I can't speak for Fred, but if *I* were Fred, *I'd* marry you.
    (*Instinctively,* THEY *run to each other and embrace*)
Oh, my Sam, my Sam! I'd marry you in a minute!

SAM (*Picks her up in his arms*)

Shhhh, shhhh, shhhh, shhhh.

JO

In a minute.
    (*Cuddled; protected; content*)
Am I heavy? No, of course I'm not heavy. What am I think-
ing of?

SAM

Shhhh, shhhh, shhhh.

JO

I think my sleepy pills are working. Shall I go to sleep right
here? Can you stand there all night?

SAM

You're not *that* light. I'll take you up.

(HE *doesn't move, beyond kissing her neck*)
I'll take you to bed.

JO
(*Giggles contentedly, interrupted by a sudden
spasm of pain, a sharp intake of breath*)
Giddyap!

SAM
Hm?

JO
Giddy*ap!* I think you'd better get me upstairs right now. I
need a couple of more pills.

SAM
(*Standing still, cuddling her*)
Not sleepy enough?

JO
Oh, I'm plenty sleepy, but if I start in screaming . . .

SAM (*Galvanized*)
O.K.! O.K.! Right!
(HE *starts with her toward the stairs*)

JO (*Clearly in pain*)
Don't jiggle me! I think I'm all coming apart! Aaaaaaaaaaa-
hhhhhhHHHHHHHH!!
(*This is a cry of beginning and rapidly growing sudden pain*)

SAM
(HE *starts up the stairs with her*)
O.K.! O.K.!

(JO *grabs at the banister, leaves* SAM'S *arms.* HE
hovers above her)

                          JO
AaaaaaahhhhHHHH!!   Sweet   Jesus!!   AaaaaaaaHHHHH-
HHHH!!

                  SAM (*Helpless*)
Let me help you.

                          JO
AaaaaaannnnnnNNHHH!
                  (SHE *waves him off*)
In a minute.
                  (*Very heavy breathing*)
AAAAARRRRrrrrrrrrrrrrrrgggggggHHHHHH!   God!   God!
God! Try to lift me!
                  (SAM *tries*)
Haaannnnh!
                  (HE *has her on her feet again. This next through
                  heavy breathing and gulping*)
It's . . . been . . . easier to . . . get me . . . to bed . . .
before.

                         SAM
                  (*Gently taking her to the top of the stairs; sooth-
                  ing, crooning*)
I'll take care of you now; I'll make you better; you'll see; I'll
put you right to bed, and take a cold cloth to your . . .

                          JO
                  (*A harsh laugh that is also a jolt of pain*)
Just . . . get me up there and lay me down. Haaaannhhh!

SAM

Sh, sh, sh. Easy, now; easy.

> (THEY *vanish from the landing. Silence for a moment.*
>
> JO *howls Offstage; then again, louder; then again, pathetic.*
>
> *Silence again.*
>
> ELIZABETH *and* OSCAR *enter the set from one side, from without the set, in that order.* OSCAR *is dressed in a suit and tie;* ELIZABETH *is dressed elegantly.*
>
> ELIZABETH *sees the audience, puts her finger to her lips, lest* THEY *start commenting, or applauding, or whatever*)

OSCAR

> (*Looking about, with some distaste*)

You say this is the place?

ELIZABETH

> (*To the audience, not urgent, not languid, but no nonsense*)

Is she alive? Are we here in time?

> (*The sound of* JO's *scream from upstairs; a brief silence, then another scream*)

ELIZABETH

> (*Still in the audience, her eyes acknowledging the sound with a brief, upward movement of her head*)

Ah yes! Well, then; we *are* in time.

> (*Turns her head slightly toward* OSCAR)

Yes; this is the place.

CURTAIN

ACT II

Morning. ELIZABETH *alone Onstage, looking out
the bay window, maybe.* SAM *comes down the
stairs, just awake, still in his sleeping gown;* HE *does
not see* ELIZABETH; HE *sees the remains of the
party's mess;* HE *takes a few more glasses, etc. As*
HE *does this,* ELIZABETH *hears him, turns, sees him.*
HE *sees her.*

ELIZABETH (*A smile; steady*)

Good morning.

SAM
(*A long silence. Finally, not loud*)

Who are *you?*

ELIZABETH

It was *late* last night; you'd already gone upstairs; there
seemed no point in . . .

SAM
(*Still not loud, but more persistent*)

Who *are* you?

ELIZABETH

There seemed no point in calling you back down don't
interrupt me, *please;* there seemed no point, from the . . .

sound of it, so to speak. So, I did not, or, *we* did not, to be more accurate.

SAM

W-we!?
> (*Looks about swiftly, sees no one*)

Who *are* you!?

ELIZABETH

Do you always leave your lights on? Glasses about? I straightened up for you a bit. If you have a fire going, do you . . . abandon it, and hope for the best? Civilizations have gone down that way, you know.

SAM (*Teeth clenched now*)

Who *are* you!?

ELIZABETH

Look at Russia! Carelessness; putting off; no other reason for the Bolsheviks. If the Czar and his boys had been a little quicker, a little more precise, Lenin wouldn't have had a chance. He'd have stayed in Zurich and taken a job teaching at some university.

SAM (*Overly polite*)

Who *are* you?

ELIZABETH

Probably would have gotten tenure—if they had tenure in those days. Don't you think it's ironic Karl Marx was a Jew? —the Soviets being so anti-Semitic, and all?

SAM

I don't believe he had Russia in mind. WHO ARE YOU!?

ELIZABETH

You don't believe he had . . . ! Is that so!

(*To the audience*)

Of course! It was probably Germany he had in mind all
along, and if it had worked out the way Marx and Engels
had it planned we would have been spared both Hitler and
Stalin. Good old Marx! Good old Engels!

(*Back to* SAM)

Or, do you think we would have had Hitler and Stalin any-
way, in some other guise—the "we-get-what-we-deserve-no-
matter-what" theory? I'm of two minds.

SAM

(*Losing patience, but still understated*)

Who are you?

ELIZABETH

Which is an odd phrase, is it not: "I'm of two minds."

(*A shift of tone to more serious, concerned*)

It sounded pretty awful up there last night. The pain, I
mean. It sounded . . . well, relentless.

SAM (*Rage coming*)

Who *are* you!?

(*To the audience*)

Who *is* this woman?

ELIZABETH

You'll be on injections soon—*she* will be, rather. I hope
you're prepared for all that—man into nurse; overseer; the
diminishment. I hope you're prepared for all that.

SAM

(*To* ELIZABETH; *threat deep in the throat*)

Who AAARRRRE you!?

ELIZABETH

(*This speech to both* SAM *and the audience*)

I remember someone, a lady who had been good to me, a lady much older than I, older than I am now and I was young; I remember there was no one else to do it all; it was on *me*; I didn't like any of it: injecting, swabbing, bathing, changing, holding close, holding her close to crush the pain out of her; picking her up—my God, no weight at all, a sack of dust—picking her up to take her to the window, so the roses and trees could get a look at her, I guess; and taking her back. "Where are you taking me," she said. "Where did you take me to, and where are you putting me?" Her eyes were open; she'd gone blind with it and I hadn't known. She hadn't said—or noticed.

(*To* SAM *alone now*)

I wonder who she was? Was she my mother? I hope you're prepared for it.

SAM (*Finally*)

WHO ARE YOU!!!???

ELIZABETH (*So calm*)

You're shouting. Who *am* I?

(*To the audience*)

The gentleman wants to know who I am.

(*To* SAM)

Well . . . who are *you?*

SAM

I'm Jo's husband; this is my house . . .

ELIZABETH

You'll wake her with your shouting. Is she still asleep? You'll wake her.

SAM
(*A quick glance above; intense, whispered*)
Dear, great God, woman, who are you!?

ELIZABETH
(*Quietly amused by* SAM'S *phrasing*)
Dear, great God, woman, who am I?
(OSCAR *enters from the library*)
Oscar? Who am I?
(*To* SAM)
This is Oscar; Oscar and I are . . . together.
(SAM *swings around to face* OSCAR, *who bows his
head slightly, smiles.* SAM *stiffens, takes a few steps
back, to have* BOTH *of them in view*)

OSCAR (*To* SAM)
Good morning, young man.
(*To* ELIZABETH)
Who *are* you? Well, ooze my widda wubby cupcake, is what-
'ums *ooze* is.

ELIZABETH (*Laughs*)
Widda *wubby* cupcake? What's a wubby?

OSCAR (*Great dignity*)
A wubby? A wubby is an adjective.
(*To* SAM)
I said: Good morning, young man.

ELIZABETH (*Some disbelief*)
An adjective?

OSCAR (*To* SAM)
It was late last night; you'd already gone upstairs; there
seemed no point in calling you back down.

(*To* ELIZABETH)

Yes; an adjective, as is widda; widda and wubby are both adjectives.

ELIZABETH

It *seems* . . . excessive.

SAM (*Quiet threat*)

I want you both out of here—whoever you are.

OSCAR (*To* SAM; *unintimidated*)

Do you always leave your lights on? Glasses about? If you have a fire going, do you . . . abandon it, and hope for the best?

ELIZABETH

We've *done* that. He pointed out, by the way, that Marx and Engels didn't have Russia in mind at all.

OSCAR (*Broad, to the audience*)

Well, everyone knows that.

ELIZABETH (*Quarrelsome*)

Not *every*one. I'm sure there are perfectly good people, walking upright and all, who have never heard of Marx and Engels—Engels certainly.

OSCAR (*To* ELIZABETH)

Impossible! A ridiculous idea!

SAM (*Flat*)

Carol.

OSCAR

Hm? Pardon?

SAM

Carol; she didn't know who Marx and Engels were.

ELIZABETH

There! You see!? A perfectly good person.

OSCAR

Who says!
                    (*To the audience*)
Who is this *Carol*, and what do we know of her? Is she to be
trusted? Would she *pretend* not to know who Marx and
Engels were?
        (SAM *is moving toward the telephone slowly, keep-
        ing his eyes on them* BOTH.
        To ELIZABETH)
Is she the sort of person who would get *pleasure* from ap-
pearing stupid?

ELIZABETH

Not Carol. Not if I know Carol.

OSCAR

Do you know Carol?

ELIZABETH (*Shrugs, giggles*)

I don't know. Show me Carol, and I'll tell you.
        (SAM *moves to the phone, begins dialing*)

OSCAR (*To* SAM)

Who are you calling? The police? What will you tell them?
What will you tell them we are? Thieves? Murderers? Relatives come to call? House inspectors? What?
        (SAM *hesitates, hangs up*)

ELIZABETH

House inspectors?

SAM (*Curiously close to tears*)

Will you *please* leave?

OSCAR

You don't even know who we *are* and you want us to leave.
(*To* ELIZABETH)
House inspectors: that's the people who inspect houses.
(*To* SAM *again*)
Don't you want to know who we are?

SAM (*Explodes*)

No! No, I don't want to know who you are! I want you out
of here! I want you out of here now!
(*Looks toward the ceiling, points*)
Damn it! My wife is very ill . . .

OSCAR (*To* SAM)

Well, why else are we here?
(*To the audience*)
Oh, I suppose there could be other reasons: a ride in the car;
a breath of fresh air; a look at how the neighborhood's
changed; the thrill of expectation—all that.

SAM (*Suspicious*)

You know Jo?

OSCAR (*To* SAM)

Why would we come here if we didn't *know* someone?
What do you think we are?

SAM (*Not to be put off*)

You know her? Tell me how you know her.

OSCAR (*To* SAM)

Look here; do you think we're house inspectors? Do we *look*
like house inspectors?

(*No reply*)

Well, maybe you don't know what house inspectors look like. They wear hats; they carry cigars; they tend toward overweight; you can turn their heads with a twenty, or a kiss. Why are you wearing that strange garment?

(SAM *becomes aware of how* HE *is dressed*)

ELIZABETH

I rather like it.

SAM (*Iron*)

It's how I dress; it's how I dress for bed.

OSCAR

Ah, then you're going to bed.

SAM

I've *been* to bed.

OSCAR

Ahhhh. Then you've just gotten *up?*

SAM (*Irritated*)

Yes!

OSCAR (*To the audience*)

I've been up for hours; I rarely sleep.

ELIZABETH (*To the audience*)

I dozed; I watched the night die.

(*Pause*)

SAM (*Fairly assertive*)

Leave!

OSCAR (*To* SAM)

What did *you* do?

ELIZABETH (*To* SAM)

Did *you* sit up? We heard the cries, and then the silence.
Did you sit up, and hold her hand until the drugs had done
their work? Did you lie down beside her then, put off the
light, and stare up into the dark? Where did you fall asleep?
Where did you wake up? Hm?

SAM (*Softly*)

Please? Leave?

ELIZABETH (*As softly; comforting*)

No.

OSCAR (*Bright; after a pause*)

Since we are not house inspectors, nor have ever been, and,
for that matter—though I speak for myself—cannot imagine
being, then we are thieves, murderers, or . . . relatives come
to call.

SAM

Please!

ELIZABETH

Be gentle, Oscar.

OSCAR

Are you very wealthy? If we are thieves, after all . . .
      (*Looks about. To the audience; wrinkles his nose*)
"Comfortable," I should think, as the definitions go. Not
much ostentation, but *still* . . . a little too obvious for "old
money," wouldn't you say? No battered greatness.

(*Back to* SAM *now*)

Where are your animals? Very rich people always have live-
stock. No, you're comfortable, nothing more.

SAM (*Heavily sarcastic*)

Sorry!

OSCAR (*Spies a print on the wall*)

What is that!?
(*Goes to it. To the audience*)
My goodness; a Jaspar Johns!
(*To* SAM *again*)
None of that Warhol shit for you, eh? Good taste! A nice
print.

SAM

Take it!

OSCAR

What! A print!? Don't be silly.

SAM

Take whatever you want. Take the stereo; take the televi-
sion; there are *three* of them, take 'em all!

ELIZABETH

Why?

SAM

Pardon?

ELIZABETH

Why are there three TVs? There aren't enough programs
for one. What happened, did they just . . . accumulate?

SAM (*Shrill*)

I'm not going to apologize for having three TV sets! Get out
of my house!

OSCAR (*To* SAM)

She wasn't suggesting you should; be calm. We don't *want*
your gadgets; next you'll offer us a microwave oven, or a
Cuisinart. Your stereo and all that stuff are for junkies and
for punks. *Look* at us; we don't even want your nice little
Jaspar Johns. We're not *thieves*. Are you relieved?

SAM

(*Very unpleasant; an edge of threat*)

No!

ELIZABETH

Nobody would offer a Cuisinart to a pair of thieves—punks
or junkies; you're being outré.

OSCAR (*To* ELIZABETH)

Well, if I were a *thief*, that would be something I would
know.

(*To* SAM)

Which proves what I said—that we are not . . . thieves.

SAM

WHAT *ARE* YOU!?

OSCAR

Well, from the original list that leaves murderers and relatives come to call.

ELIZABETH

Not necessarily a happy choice—though I don't know your
circle.

SAM

WHAT THE FUCK DO I HAVE TO DO TO GET YOU
OUT OF HERE!!??
(*A silence*)

OSCAR (*Quietly*)
Guess who we are, for beginners. And you're so close.

SAM (*Sits; rather defeated*)
All right; who *are* you? Who *are* you?

OSCAR (*Going to him; gentle*)
We are not murderers, nor are we thieves . . .

ELIZABETH
Nor are we house inspectors . . .

OSCAR (*The end of a fairy tale*)
Then we are relatives, come to call.

SAM (*Weary*)
You're relatives; good. You're . . .
(*Looks at* OSCAR)
. . . no, you're not! You're not a relative at all!

OSCAR
Oh?

SAM (*Gestures*)
Well . . . *look* at you.
(ELIZABETH *chuckles throughout*)

OSCAR
Look at me? Am I dressed oddly? Do my clothes offend?

SAM
(*Knows what's being done, but can't fight it*)

No.

OSCAR

Am I too tall?

SAM

No.

OSCAR

Too *short*.

SAM

No; no.

OSCAR

Am I too old?

SAM

No.

OSCAR (*Feigning confusion*)

Too young?

SAM

No, of course not.

OSCAR

Too thin, then.

SAM

No!

OSCAR

Too fat?

SAM

NO!

OSCAR

Is it my way of speaking? Am I too . . . refined?

SAM

NO!

OSCAR

Am I . . . too rich?

SAM

How would I know?

OSCAR

Too poor?

SAM

How would I *know!?*

OSCAR

Well, it *is* a puzzle. What could it *be?* Could it . . . oh, my
goodness, I think I have it! Is it . . .
          (HE *leans over and whispers in* SAM's *ear*)

SAM (*Listens, nods*)

Yup; that's it; you got it.

OSCAR
          (*To* ELIZABETH; *mock distress*)

It's that I'm . . .
                    (*Stage whisper*)

Too black.

ELIZABETH (*Absurd!*)

Too what! Too black!?

OSCAR

It would appear so.

SAM

No offense.

OSCAR

Given or taken?

(*To* ELIZABETH)

It would appear so. Too black. What did Mister Blake say?
. . . "But I am black, as if bereav'd of light."

(*Hamming*)

"And, I am black, but, oh, my soul is white!" Some shit like
that.

SAM

I said: no offense.

OSCAR (*Suddenly friendly*)

And none taken, white boy; none taken. Well, now, if I am
too black to be a relative—though there's a nigger in many
a woodpile, and don't you forget it!—then *I* must be a
friend. Perhaps Elizabeth here is a relative.

SAM (*Almost a mumble*)

Well, I'm sure Jo will be very happy to see you.

ELIZABETH (*To* SAM; *arch*)

Was that sarcasm?

(*To* OSCAR)

Oscar, did that sound like sarcasm to you, to your black ears?

s a m (*Weary*)

It was not sarcasm.

o s c a r

It sounded like it to me.
            (*Smiles unpleasantly. To the audience*)
But then, so much does.

s a m (*Frustration, fatigue*)

It was *not* sarcasm; I'm very *tired*; I sat *up*; I'm sure Jo will
be very happy to *see* you. God! Let it *go!*

o s c a r (*Rather cheerful; to* sam)

Be nice to this lady; she has come a distance.

s a m

(*Trying to be conversational*)
What, uh . . . what kind of relative . . . uh, *are* you?

e l i z a b e t h

(*Surprised, but gracious*)
Why . . . I'm Jo's mother.
            (*Considerable pause*)

s a m

(*As if* he *hadn't heard properly*)
Pardon?

e l i z a b e t h (*Patient*)

I'm Jo's mother.

o s c a r

(*To* sam, *when* he *fails to respond*)
Her *mother!* Jo's *mother!*

(SAM *begins to laugh, quietly, shaking his head;*
the laughter is close to crying.
To SAM)
Is that the laughter to keep from crying?
                    (*To* ELIZABETH; *chipper*)
Do you think that's the laughter to keep from crying?

                    S A M (*A heavy sigh*)
O.K., gang; out! Whoever you are . . . get out.

                    E L I Z A B E T H (*Rather harsh*)
I'm Jo's mother, come from Dubuque!

                    O S C A R
The Lady from Dubuque; this is the lady from Dubuque;
Jo's mother!

                    E L I Z A B E T H (*A hand up*)
Never mind, Oscar.

                    O S C A R (*To* SAM)
Jo's mother; from Dubuque. What's the *matter* with you!?
Kiss her!

                    S A M
                (*Anger through the fatigue*)
You are *not* Jo's mother.
                    (*To the audience*)
She is *not* Jo's mother.
                    (*To* ELIZABETH *and* OSCAR)
JESUS CHRIST, HAVE SOME COMPASSION, WILL
YOU!?

                    O S C A R
                (*Very offhand; to the audience*)
I wonder why he's resisting?

ELIZABETH (*Sighs; rises*)

I wonder why we're *talking?* Clearly it's no use. It's time I
went upstairs.

SAM

(*Frightened, but standing his ground*)

You're both crazy; both of you, you're crazy.

ELIZABETH

(*Dismissing him with a little gesture*)

Oh . . . fiddlesticks! Oscar, will you stay down here with
this young man?

SAM

YOU STAY AWAY FROM JO!!

ELIZABETH (*Amused*)

Stay away from her? Not let her hug me? Where do you
think she learned it all? Do you think she put her arms
around nobody before *you?* What gall! We all have ante-
cedents, and we all can be replaced. Keep that in mind.

SAM

You stay away from her!

ELIZABETH

Why don't you be a good boy and go in the kitchen now
and make us all a hearty breakfast?

OSCAR

(*Wringing his hands; smacking his lips*)

Corn pone, grits . . .

ELIZABETH

A Sunday breakfast! Steaming pots of coffee, rolls, and eggs,
and slabs of ham. Jo used to love that, back on the farm.

S A M (*Contemptuous*)

You were never on a farm in your life.

O S C A R (*Almost to himself*)

Iowa *is* farm country.

S A M

(*To the audience; desperate*)

Jo's mother lives in New Jersey!

E L I Z A B E T H

(*After* SHE *and* OSCAR BOTH *hoot*)

New Jersey!? Do you mean this person you're trying to pass off as Jo's mother comes from . . . New Jersey?

S A M

What are *you* . . . some kind of *comic?*

E L I Z A B E T H (*Suddenly very sober*)

No; very serious, and very concerned. Will I find the bedroom to the right?

(SHE *starts toward the stairs;* SAM *moves to a blocking position*)

S A M

You stay where you are.

E L I Z A B E T H (*Stone*)

I have come home for my daughter's dying. Get out of my way.

S A M

(*An almost-whispered litany*)

You are not Jo's mother, you have never been on a farm, Jo was not raised on a farm, you are not from Dubuque; you are not a relative and this black man is not a friend.

ELIZABETH

This black man here, who is probably very rapidly becoming
what you say—*not* a friend—is wise and quick and shockingly
strong.

OSCAR (*Smiles*)

Imperial Japanese Army; World War Two.

ELIZABETH

I think he will help me if I need him.

OSCAR (*Mock ecstatic*)

Oh, Elizabeth! Anything!

SAM (*Kind of punchy*)

You were *not* in the Japanese Army in World War Two.

OSCAR (*To the audience*)

I wonder where I learned my love for uncooked fish?

ELIZABETH

Not to mention your command of the martial arts.
(*To* SAM, *with a charming smile*)
He'll have you unconscious just like that.

OSCAR

(*Bows in the Japanese manner; to* SAM)
Ohayoo gozaimasu. Ogenki desuka?
(SAM *doesn't respond*)
Do shimashita ka?
(*To* ELIZABETH)
What's the matter with *him?*

ELIZABETH (*Shrugs*)

He doesn't know Japanese; he's lost face.

(*To* sam)

Don't fret; it's not a required language yet. Just like that!
Unconscious, flat on your back. *So-o,* if you will let me pass
. . .

> (sam *blocks the stairway;* oscar *moves slightly;* sam
> *includes him in his defense posture—arms angled in*
> *front, hands as barriers, eyes flickering from* one *to*
> *the* other)

s a m (*Steel*)

Stay away from me, you crazy people!

o s c a r
(*Karate pose; to* sam)
HIIIIIIIIYYYYYEEEEAAAAAHHH!!!

s a m

Oh, my *God!*

e l i z a b e t h (*Purring*)

Would you care to negotiate, young man?

s a m
(*Not taking his eyes off* oscar)
Would I care to . . . would I *what?*

e l i z a b e t h

You have a woman upstairs. You *say* she is your wife; *I* say
she is my daughter. Surely we can negotiate this.

o s c a r (*A sinister echo*)
Surely you can negotiate this.

s a m (*Quietly; to* elizabeth)

Who *are* you? *Really?*

ELIZABETH (*Gentle*)

Who are *you? Really?*

(A *long silence;* SAM *looks at them* BOTH)

SAM (*Finally; very calm*)

I'll go upstairs, and I'll talk to Jo. I'll wake her if she's asleep, and I'll tell her what's been happening; she won't believe me, but I'll tell her.

ELIZABETH

Bring her down.

SAM (*Adamant*)

I'll *tell* her.

ELIZABETH (*Harder*)

You'll bring her down; that's our negotiation. Negotiation's over; I'll call off the dogs.

(SHE *turns her back on* SAM)

OSCAR (*Quite amused*)

You'll call off the *what?*

ELIZABETH (*Laughs*)

Oh, hush!

SAM

If she says she'll come—if she believes what I tell her and she says she'll come—maybe you'll be gone. You aren't really here, are you? I'll come back down and you'll be gone?

OSCAR

Gone?

ELIZABETH (*A harsh laugh*)

Oh, *we* exist. Worry about your*self.*

SAM
(*Starts backing up the stairs*)

I exist; *you* don't.

ELIZABETH (*Lazy*)

Well, we'll see.

(*Amused*)

Oh! While you're up there . . . *do* change out of that silly getup.

SAM (*Near tears*)

It's how I dress; it's how I dress for bed!
(HE *hesitates, then rushes up the stairs and Offstage*)

ELIZABETH (*Convulsed*)

It's how I dress!

(*To the audience*)

It's how I dress for bed!
(THEY BOTH *laugh greatly;* ELIZABETH *holds her hands out, palms upward;* OSCAR *slaps them in an exaggerated imitation of street blacks. Their backs are to the entry hallway*)

OSCAR (*To* ELIZABETH; *sober*)

He doubts you.

(*To the audience*)

He doubts her.

ELIZABETH (*To* OSCAR; *to herself*)

I know.

(*To the audience*)

How can he doubt me? How can he doubt me?
(LUCINDA *and* EDGAR *enter from the hallway,* LU-CINDA *leading the way*)

LUCINDA (With enthusiasm)

Surprise! Surprise! Sur . . .

    (SHE sees ELIZABETH and OSCAR, finishes it, deflated
    and cautious)

. . . prise; surprise.

EDGAR

Well . . .

LUCINDA (To ELIZABETH)

Good . . . good morning.

ELIZABETH (A grand hostess)

Good morning; I'm Jo's mother . . . and you must be
. . . ?

LUCINDA
(Nonplussed; self-conscious)

Jo's . . . what? Jo's mother?
(Fairly faint)
I'm Lucinda and this is Edgar.

EDGAR (Uncomfortable)

Hi.

ELIZABETH (Grand)

How do you do? This is Oscar.
(OSCAR bows)
Oscar is black.

LUCINDA

I noticed.

EDGAR

Yes; so did I.

(*More formal*)
Where's Sam? Where's Jo?

ELIZABETH
(*Rather offhand, if final*)
They are . . . upstairs.

EDGAR (*Puzzled*)
Thank you.

LUCINDA
(*Nervously, to fill the gap*)
So. You're Jo's mother.

ELIZABETH
Yes; I am.

LUCINDA
I never would have guessed! I mean . . . you're not at all
what I imagined.

ELIZABETH
Oh?

LUCINDA
We've never had the pleasure, of course—you're something
of a recluse; a famous name in these parts, but nothing more.

ELIZABETH
Oh?

LUCINDA
(*Not helped by* ELIZABETH)
You . . . you live with your *sister* now.

ELIZABETH

I . . . move about all the time.

LUCINDA (*Confused*)

Oh?

ELIZABETH (*A short laugh*)

Well! One may *be* from Dubuque . . .

OSCAR

Iowa; Dubuque, Iowa.

LUCINDA

Du . . . buque?

ELIZABETH

But certainly one *roams:* Dubuque is not everything.

LUCINDA (*Puzzled*)

Sam says you live with your sister, couple of hours from here.
(*With an uncomfortable look at* OSCAR)
With your older sister; you two sort of . . . look out for one
another.

ELIZABETH (*Laughs*)

Sam says that?
(*To* OSCAR)
What can Sam mean?

LUCINDA (*To* EDGAR; *uncertainly*)

I'm sure that's what we've been told?

OSCAR

Sam's a joker all right.

LUCINDA (*Quite puzzled*)

You never go out; you stay in.

(*Nudges* EDGAR)

Edgar! Help me!

(*A nervous laugh*)

And you're very tiny, and terribly thin.

ELIZABETH (*Crystal laughter*)

You must have me confused with someone else—a great aunt, perhaps. I have my Christmas in Switzerland, though, to be completely candid with you, I spent *one* December in Peru.

LUCINDA

Pe . . . ru?

OSCAR (*Helpful*)

The country.

LUCINDA

And . . . and you have pink hair.

ELIZABETH (*Greatly amused*)

Pink hair!? On purpose?!

(*To the audience*)

Pink hair!?

OSCAR

Clearly you have Elizabeth confused in your mind with someone else—some defective or eccentric somewhere, some embarrassment your friends are taking care to see is . . .

LUCINDA (*Close to hysteria*)

Well, I must be mistaken! Edgar? Jo's mother is clearly not a recluse; I mean . . . *look* at her: she does not have pink hair, nor is she tiny.

EDGAR

No.

OSCAR (*Mollifying*)
She's not . . . gigantic, of course.

LUCINDA
No! We can *see* that!

OSCAR
She is what you might refer to as a normal-size mother.

LUCINDA
Yes! Yes! Still . . .

EDGAR
Oh, come on, Lucinda! For Christ's sake!

LUCINDA
(*Making ineffectual little slaps at* EDGAR)
Don't *be* that way to me! Give me one good reason why
Sam, or Jo—Jo, for heaven's sake—give me one good reason
why Jo would pretend her mother is a tiny, pink-haired re-
cluse, living—

ELIZABETH
BECAUSE!!
(*Silence; attention is paid. Quietly; to end the matter*)
Because . . . there are things you would not be expected to
understand.
(*A long silence*)

EDGAR (*Finally*)
Right.

LUCINDA

Oh.

(*Pause*)

All right; if you say so.

(*To save it*)

Besides, I knew it wasn't true from the beginning—New Jersey, pink hair, and all!

EDGAR

(*To* LUCINDA; *humoring her*)

You get everything so mixed up! Can't put one over on you, eh Lu?

(LUCINDA *starts to reply, but* FRED *and* CAROL *appear in the hallway*)

FRED

(*Just as* HE *comes into view,* CAROL *following*)

Hey? Anybody up?

OSCAR (*To the audience*)

My gracious! It *is* a party!

FRED

Anybody . . .

EDGAR

Fred! For Christ's sake!

FRED (*Takes it all in*)

. . . hey, what's all this!

ELIZABETH

(*Still the grand hostess*)

Good morning! I'm Jo's mother, and you must be . . . ?

FRED (*Some urgency; to* EDGAR)
Where's Sam? Where's Jo?

EDGAR
It's O.K. They're upstairs.

FRED (*To* LUCINDA *and* EDGAR)
What the hell are you two doing here?

CAROL
(*Peering at* ELIZABETH *and* OSCAR)
We in the right house, Fred?

FRED
(*Not really unpleasant; preoccupied*)
Shut up, Carol.

ELIZABETH
How do you do!—whoever you may be.

CAROL
I don't think we're in the right house, Fred.

FRED (*To* EDGAR)
What the hell are you two *doing* here?

EDGAR
Lucinda wanted to make it up with Jo . . . for last night
. . . out on the lawn.

FRED
Oh.

ELIZABETH
And you?

(*To the audience*)
Don't these people answer questions?

FRED

Hunh?

ELIZABETH (*Too precise; to* FRED)
And . . . you! To what do we owe the pleasure? Are you
friends of my daughter as well?

CAROL (*To* FRED; *sotto voce*)
Is that Jo's *mother?*

FRED

Shut up, Carol.
(*To* ELIZABETH)
Well, Carol here and I, we decided to get married—you
know, what the hell!—and so we wanted to tell Sam and Jo,
and . . .

ELIZABETH
Well, well; congratulations.

EDGAR
How *about* that! Hey!

CAROL (*Shrugging twice*)
You know: what the hell!

LUCINDA
(*Badly disguised distaste*)
Oh; you two are getting married; how wonderful.

FRED
Ah, fuck off, Lucinda.

LUCINDA (*Defend me!*)
Edgar?

EDGAR
Do what Fred says, hunh?
(*To* FRED *and* CAROL)
That's swell, kids; that is just swell.

OSCAR (*To the audience*)
I haven't heard "swell" in a very long time. Can you remember when you last heard "swell"?

ELIZABETH (*To* FRED *and* CAROL)
This is Oscar. Oscar is black.

FRED (*None too pleasant*)
I noticed. How come your friend is black?

ELIZABETH
How come he's what?

FRED
Black.

ELIZABETH
Black!? (*To* OSCAR) How come you're black?

OSCAR
Because my mammy and my pappy was black.

CAROL (*A smile*)
Fred's a redneck.

ELIZABETH (*To* CAROL)
Isn't that nice?

(*To* FRED)

Have you been one long?

FRED (*A cold smile*)

It comes and goes.

OSCAR
(*To the audience; quite chummy*)

I met a foreign lady once—Belgian, I think—nice lady, very solicitous, kept asking me questions about something she insisted was called the Ku-Ku-Klan. Nice lady.

(*To* FRED; *very pleasant*)

Are you a member of the Ku-Ku-Klan?

FRED (*Tight smile*)

What do you want to bet?

CAROL

Aw, come on! Fred's a pussycat.
(OSCAR *laughs, unpleasantly.*
A *silence*)

LUCINDA

Jo's mother here has come all the way from Dubuque to pay Jo a visit, Jo being sick and all . . .

FRED

Dubuque?

ELIZABETH

I am from Dubuque; I am the lady from Dubuque.
(*Specifically to* EDGAR)

Though I have not just come from there. I was in . . . uh . . .

(*Clearly* SHE'S *improvising*)
St. Paul de Vence, on my way from Paris down to . . .

OSCAR (*Right in*)

Rome; Rome, Italy.

ELIZABETH

Thank you.

(*To the* OTHERS)

I do not . . . summer in Dubuque.

CAROL (*An aside, to* FRED)

Who is this *person?*

LUCINDA (*Effusive*)

Jo's mother is not at all what we had been led to believe.

ELIZABETH (*To* FRED *and* CAROL)

Tiny, pink-haired, reclusive, living on the dole somewhere
with a sister.

LUCINDA

No; well; you *see!* Not at all what we'd imagined. The idea
of Sam leading us on like that . . .

CAROL (*Merely curious*)

Are those pearls real?

ELIZABETH

Real what?

CAROL (*Hostile*)

Real pearl!

FRED

Shut up, Carol.

CAROL
(*Quite angry, but not loud*)
Don't tell me to shut up all the time. You want me to marry
you? Just come off it about shut up all the time. We aren't
married *yet*, so *watch* it!

ELIZABETH (*Gracious*)
I don't know; they were given me; but I've no reason to
assume they're other than that which they pretend to be.
(SAM *has appeared at the top of the stairs;* HE *has
changed into a shirt and trousers*)

SAM
Unlike some people I could mention.

FRED

Hey! Sam!
(SAM *slowly descends the stairs*)

LUCINDA (*Nervous; sing-song*)
You're having a *party*! You may not have *known* it, but
you're having a *party*! Fred and Carol are getting—

FRED
Hey, Sam, you hear about Carol and me? We're getting
married.

EDGAR

Morning, Sam.

ELIZABETH
I've been entertaining your friends; they're charming, abso-
lutely charming. Oscar and I have been enthralled.

CAROL (*Sheepish*)

Hi, Sam.

LUCINDA

We've gotten to know Jo's mother here. We were so surprised; we came in, more or less on tiptoe, and . . .

FRED

Carol and I are getting married, Sam.
    (SAM *is at the bottom of the stairs now.* HE *has not
taken his eyes off* ELIZABETH *the entire journey
down.* HE *stops in front of her*)

OSCAR (*To* ELIZABETH; *cooing*)

See how he loves you already; he can't take his eye off of you.

FRED

Sam? You O.K.?

EDGAR

Sam?

OSCAR (*To the audience*)

See how he stares at her! See the intensity of his gaze! *This*
is passion!

FRED (*Concerned*)

Sam?

SAM

    (*Waves them off; to* ELIZABETH, *precise, quiet,
formal, controlled*)
I spoke to Jo; I told her . . . you two had arrived; I told her
who you said you were.

ELIZABETH

And?

SAM

She's getting up; she's coming down; and that will be the end
of it.

LUCINDA (*To* EDGAR *and* CAROL)

I don't understand what's going on!

EDGAR

Sam? You O.K.?

SAM

It's . . .
(*Bravura; slightly hysterical*)
. . . it's all right, folks, it's . . . all . . . just wonderful.
This . . . this lady here and her—and this one—the two of
them were waiting for me when I came downstairs this morning. *This* one—this lady here—says she's Jo's *mother.* I don't
know who *this* one thinks *he* is. *I* say she's *not* Jo's mother.

FRED (*Laughs*)

Oh, come on, now!

SAM

No, now! Don't laugh!

FRED (*Harsh laugh*)

Nobody pretends to be somebody's *mother!*

SAM
(*Contained, but the hysteria is underneath*)
I know! Nobody pretends to be somebody's mother!

(*Still the hysteria underneath;* to FRED, CAROL,
EDGAR, LUCINDA, *and the audience*)
THIS IS NOT JO'S MOTHER!

FRED (*To* SAM; *sighs*)
O.K., Sam, what are you doing—playing some kind of game?
Didn't you have enough last night? What kind of game are
you *playing*?

SAM
(*To* FRED; *sputtering; exploding*)
Am *I* playing! What kind of game am *I* playing!?

FRED
You got a sick wife upstairs, her mother comes home—with
a friend, or something—and all you can do is make jokes?

SAM (*Beside himself*)
All I can do is . . . ? THIS IS NOT JO'S MOTHER!!

FRED
Of course it's Jo's mother! Who the hell else is it!?

SAM (*About to burst*)
I don't know! I don't *know* who it is!

FRED
(*Weary of it, dismissing* SAM)
Oh, for God's sake!

SAM
I DON'T KNOW WHO IT *IS*!
(*A silence*)

LUCINDA (*Brisk; slaps her knees*)
Well! Who's for a good pot of coffee?

FRED

Fuck that! Let's open the bar.
> (HE *moves toward the bar*)

SAM (*Fury*)

NOBODY!!
> (*Pause*)

NOBODY!!

OSCAR
> (*Into a silence; to the audience*)

Well, I suppose that's natural—a man who would deny his
wife's own mother could not be expected to provide his
friends with a cup of coffee or a drink.

SAM
> (*Turns to* OSCAR, *fist cocked*)

Look, you fucker!

OSCAR
> (*To* SAM; *loud, authoritative*)

I warn you!
> (SAM *hesitates;* OSCAR *assumes a karate pose*)

I warn you; I have my black belt.
> (*An aside, to* ELIZABETH)

Which should come as no surprise.
> (OSCAR *holds out his palm;* ELIZABETH *slaps it, in an*
> *exaggerated imitation of street blacks*)

SAM
> (*Turns away in disgust and defeat*)

Ah, for Christ's sake!

CAROL (*To* SAM)

Your mother-in-law's quite a card; so's her friend there.

(*To* ELIZABETH *and* OSCAR)
You're quite a pair.

ELIZABETH (*Queen Elizabeth*)
Thank you, *thank* you.

SAM (*Weary; ironic*)
You're quite a pair, too, Carol, but she isn't my mother-in-
law.

LUCINDA (*Dismissing him*)
Oh, really, Sam.

SAM (*Hopeless*)
She's *not*.

FRED
Bullshit!

SAM (*To* CAROL)
You really gonna marry that sonofabitch?

CAROL
(*Argumentative, if not enthusiastic*)
He'll *do!*

SAM
Which says as much about you as it does about him! Congratulations to you both!

FRED (*Quietly; to* SAM)
Fuck yourself; and no kidding. Just go fuck yourself.

ELIZABETH (*Amused; above it all*)
Bicker, bicker! This is not the *time* for it.

SAM (*To* ELIZABETH; *enraged*)

You! You shut up!

FRED (*Disgust*)

Look, this is a nice lady you're talking to.

SAM

(*Loud; looking down at the floor*)

SHUT UP! SHUT UP! SHUT UP!

(JO *appears at the top of the stairs. Suddenly shaken and in tears, pathetic*)

Please! Please! All of you! Shut . . . up! Just . . . shut . . . up. Please!

(*A silence*)

OSCAR (*To the audience*)

The view from above, to the pit below.

ELIZABETH (*Gentle, deferential*)

The man has asked for silence; give it to him.

OSCAR

(*Hands out, fingers wide; still to the audience*)

Let there be silence; shhhhhhhhhhhh.

JO (*Tentative*)

Sam?

SAM (*A whisper*)

Jo?

(*All eyes go to* JO. ELIZABETH *moves slightly so that* SHE *is near the foot of the stairs*)

JO

(*As* SAM *makes to move toward her*)

No; I'll make it down; don't anyone move.

(SHE *begins her descent, her eyes on* ELIZABETH.
Halfway down SHE *gasps in pain, nearly crumbles*)

SAM

JO!

JO
(*Straightening again; smiling*)

No one *help* me.
(JO *completes her descent, save two steps; her eyes
are still on* ELIZABETH; SHE *stops where* SHE *is*)

ELIZABETH (*Gentle; a smile*)

Good morning.

JO
(*After a pause; quiet, noncommittal*)

Good morning.

OSCAR
(*To* ELIZABETH, *his eyes on* JO)

You never told me how lovely she was—so pure, so fragile:
scented air.

SAM

These are the two who have come, Jo. This is the woman
claims to be your mother. Tell her, Jo; tell her you don't
know her.

ELIZABETH (*Gentle*)

Good morning.

SAM

Tell her she has no right to come into our house and pretend
to be what she is not.
(JO *has a spasm of pain;* SHE *moans*)

LUCINDA (*True grief*)

Oh, Jo!

OSCAR

Take her in your arms, Elizabeth; ease her; hold her close.

SAM (*To* OSCAR)

YOU STAY OUT OF THIS!!
(JO *grimaces; a cry escapes her*)

ELIZABETH

Come to me.

SAM (*Through his teeth*)

You stay away from her!

JO (*Looks at* SAM; *quietly*)

Sam?

SAM (*Begging*)

Tell her, Jo. Tell her we don't know her.
(JO's *eyes return to* ELIZABETH)

ELIZABETH

Come to me, now. It's time to hold you close, to rock you in
my arms.

JO (*Timid*)

Rock me?

ELIZABETH (*Soothing*)

Hold you, rock you, take you to my breast.

SAM

NO!

ELIZABETH (*A litany*)

Come, let me stroke your forehead, comb your hair, wash
you, lay you down and tell you stories . . .

SAM

JO! NO!

ELIZABETH

Protect you from the dark and from the thunder?

JO (*A little girl*)

Protect me?

SAM

NO!

ELIZABETH (*Smiles*)

From the dark and from the thunder.

JO

Make it better?

SAM (*Agony*)

Oh, Jo!

ELIZABETH (*So tender, gentle*)

Make it better? What have I come for? Come to me.

SAM (*A howl of pain*)

NOOOOOoooooOOOOOO!

(*Finally, with tears and a great helpless smile,* JO
rushes into ELIZABETH's *arms; their embrace is almost a tableau, so involved is it with pressing together*)

ELIZABETH (*To the audience*)

And they wonder who I am.

SAM (*To his* FRIENDS)

No! NO! That is not Jo's mother! Believe me! BELIEVE
ME!!

(*But* THEY *have either turned away, are looking
away in embarrassment, or are regarding* SAM *with
sadness*)

NO! NO!

(HE *looks about and sees it is hopeless, but* HE *persists, in rage and tears*)

NO!

(*Pause*)

NO!

(*Pause*)

NO!

OSCAR (*Quietly; gently*)

Oh, yes. Yesyesyesyes. Oh, yes.

SAM

(*Fully in tears; quietly, desperate; to the audience*)

Believe me; this is not Jo's mother.

OSCAR

(*Quiet victory statement, to* SAM)

Oh yes she is.

SAM

(*In a final attempt to reverse the situation; to*
ELIZABETH)

NO!!

(SAM *lunges at* ELIZABETH, *to wrest* JO *from her.
As quick as lightning,* OSCAR *intercedes*)

OSCAR *(Grappling with* SAM)

I said . . . YES!

(To FRED *and* EDGAR)

Help me with him!
>   (JO *cries out in pain.*
>   FRED *and* EDGAR *come to help.*
>   SAM *and* OSCAR: *overlapping)*

SAM

No! No!

OSCAR

Yes, I said!

SAM

No! Jo!

OSCAR

Hold him for me. Hold him.
>   (FRED *and* EDGAR *each grab one of* SAM's *arms.*
>   OSCAR *touches* SAM *on the neck and* HE *is instantly*
>   *unconscious)*

OSCAR

Ease him down.
>   (SAM, *unconscious, slips to the floor)*

EDGAR

How did you do that?
>   (FRED *ties* SAM's *hands behind him with his belt)*

OSCAR

There is a nerve there, in the neck; a little pressure in the
proper spot . . . and all the woes are gone, the troubles slip
away . . . and peace descends. Off you go, to the dreap and
deemless.

EDGAR

Will he be all right?

OSCAR

He'll be all right. I can wake him . . .
(*Finger snap*)
. . . just like that.

FRED (*Having tied* SAM *up*)

I tied him up.

OSCAR

You did!? So you did. Those are splendid knots. Really first
rate. He must be *very* grateful to you.

FRED

Bastard hates me.

OSCAR (*Mollifying*)

Weeeellll, you've tied him up very nicely, nonetheless. A
regular package.

FRED (*None too pleasant*)

That's not a bad idea: *mail* him somewhere.

OSCAR (*Bright idea!*)

We could send him to New Jersey! He could visit those
mysterious ladies.

LUCINDA (*Amused*)

It would serve him right—hitting away like that!

EDGAR
(*To* ELIZABETH; *truly puzzled*)

God, the way he just . . . went at you.

LUCINDA

I've never seen such a thing! Really!
(*To* ELIZABETH)
Weren't you scared?

ELIZABETH (*Rather startled*)

Scared!? Why, no.

FRED

He was afraid to go after . . .
(*Gestures*)
. . . this one here.

EDGAR

Well, with good reason!
(*To* OSCAR)
Where did you learn all that . . .
(*Imitates* OSCAR's *judo*)
. . . all that . . . ?

OSCAR

Foreign Legion.

EDGAR

You were in the Foreign . . . ? No.

OSCAR (*Shrugs*)

All right.
(*To the audience*)
Then I *wasn't* in the Foreign Legion. *I* don't care.

JO (*A spasm alerts her*)

What's happening? What's . . .

ELIZABETH (*Soothes*)

Shhhhhh; shhhhhhhh; nothing.

(JO *becomes comatose again*)

FRED (*Regards* SAM)

I think he looks good this way. Perfect packaging.

CAROL (*Snorts; shakes her head*)

Hunh!

FRED

What's the matter with *you?*

CAROL

Sooner or later you're going to have to untie him, you know.

FRED

Yeah? So?

CAROL (*Shrugs*)

Sooner or later you're going to have to untie him; or Jo's going to get with it, and you're going to have to let him *go*.

FRED

SO!?

CAROL

So . . . *then* you're going to have to explain why you tied him up!

FRED (*Exasperated*)

I tied him up . . . you saw why I tied him up!

LUCINDA (*After a crystal laugh*)

Really, Carol!

EDGAR (*Puzzled*)
Who should we have tied up, Jo's mother here?

CAROL (*A small smile*)
Who?

JO (*An echo*)
Who?

ELIZABETH (*A bit loud*)
Tied *me* up!? Why me?
(*To the audience*)
Why would anyone tie *me* up?

OSCAR (*Generally*)
Perhaps she meant *me*.
(*To the audience*)
People are always tying coons up for one reason or another,
though less *these* days than . . .
(*Smiles*)
. . . times of yore?

CAROL
(*Speculative; not giving an inch*)
Well, it *could* be because I'm crazy . . .

FRED
Yeah! It could be because you're crazy!

CAROL (*Dubious*)
Yeah; could be; or it could be because I'm an outsider . . .

FRED
So why don't you shut up?!

CAROL (*Pursuing her logic*)

Or maybe it isn't either one; maybe it's just a feeling. Why are you all in such a rush? Why doesn't anybody believe *Sam?*

LUCINDA (*Laughs*)

Oh, really, Carol!

FRED (*Furious*)

For Christ's sake, why don't you just . . . go into the kitchen and make some coffee, or something!? Why don't you do something useful around here?

CAROL

What am *I!?* Some sort of a colored maid, or something?
(*To* OSCAR)
No offense.

OSCAR (*To* CAROL; *smooth*)

Oh, none taken!

FRED (*As* CAROL *doesn't move*)

Will you get your ass in there!?

CAROL

O.K.! O.K.! For Christ's sake!
(SHE *sweeps out, muttering*)

FRED

Good girl, Carol; just gotta goose her a little bit.

OSCAR (*To the audience*)

And I haven't heard *that* word, *either*, in a coon's age.

FRED (*Eyes narrowing a little*)

What word? Girl?

LUCINDA (*Slaps her knees, rises*)
I'll make toast; I'll make buttered toast.

ELIZABETH (*To* LUCINDA)
That will be heaven.
(LUCINDA *smiles, exits*)
Won't that be heaven, Oscar?

OSCAR
(*Considers it; to* ELIZABETH)
Well, it will be *toast*.

FRED (*At the bar again*)
You drinking, Edgar?

EDGAR
No thanks, Fred; not this early.

FRED
(*Pretending to be offended*)
Oh, I see; well; pardon *me*.

EDGAR
(*For fear of having offended*)
Of course. I'm not getting married.

FRED
Oh? Why not?

EDGAR
Because I'm already . . . I just don't want a drink, Fred.

FRED (*To* ELIZABETH *and* OSCAR)
I don't suppose either of you drinks in the morning, either.

OSCAR

No, no.

ELIZABETH

Certainly not.

FRED
(*Moves over to* SAM, *contemplates him*)
You want a drink, Sambo? A little Scotch with a straw?
Sniff it, maybe?
(*To* EDGAR)
Sambo doesn't seem to answer.

EDGAR (*Glum*)
Well, maybe *he's* not getting married, *either*.

FRED (*Cheerful*)
Well, *I* am. Fuck ya all!
(*Toasts*)

JO (*Dreamy*)
Who's getting married?

ELIZABETH
Fred is; Fred's getting married.

FRED (*Loud*)
I'm marrying Carol, Jo.

JO (*Thinks, shakes her head*)
Terrible idea.
(*Subsides.*
LUCINDA *appears in the hallway, spoons in hand*)

LUCINDA
Edgar! Come help with the tray! Don't be a bump!
(SHE *revanishes*)

EDGAR (*Fairly weary; rises*)
O.K. O.K.

ELIZABETH
A what? A bump?

EDGAR (*Exiting*)
As in on a log; a bump on a log; I shouldn't be a bump on
a log.

OSCAR
(*In the small silence as* EDGAR *exits; to the audience*)
Quaint.

JO
(*To* ELIZABETH; *in confidence*)
I've told Fred a dozen times; I've been subtle, but I've told
him—"Don't marry Carol."

ELIZABETH
Shhhh, shhh, shhh.

JO
And I've told Carol—"Don't marry Fred." Maybe nobody
ever heard me; maybe nobody listens. I hurt.

ELIZABETH
Let me hold you.

JO
Fred is a terrible person.

ELIZABETH
(*Smiles, to* FRED, *shrugs*)
Shhh; let me hold you.

JO
He is . . .
(SHE *smiles at her phrasing*)
. . . unworthy of human solicitude.
(*Gasps*)
I really *hurt.*

FRED (*Slams his drink down*)
I gotta go take a dump!
(HE *starts out*)

ELIZABETH (*Calm*)
Do you say that to offend us?

FRED (*Daring her*)
What!?

ELIZABETH
(*Will not be drawn in; smiles*)
Or is it anger? Has Jo made you angry, and are you going to
punish us all? Are you a showoff, or a boor, or is Jo right on
the mark, and are you . . . "unworthy of human solicitude"?

FRED
I'm just plain dirt common; ask Jo.
(HE *exits*)

OSCAR
Well, he is nothing if not honest, eh?
(OSCAR *wanders*)
Are you happy with the decor?

ELIZABETH (*Casual*)

I would do something else about the carpet, I think, or put
rugs down. How's the library?

OSCAR

Very masculine—heavy leather, dark woods. What would
you expect? Oh! The TV set has doors, which close; they
match the other wood.

ELIZABETH (*Delighted; giggles*)

It doesn't! They don't!
(*To* JO)
Oh, Jo! You are a *good* girl!

JO (*Vague*)

What have I *done?*

ELIZABETH

You're a good wife. You make a beautiful home.
(CAROL *enters*)

OSCAR

Very good, "Mother," very good.

ELIZABETH

Do be a help.

OSCAR

What more can I *do?* I am civil to people I cannot abide, I
function as an encyclopedia . . .

CAROL

You knock people out.

OSCAR (*Recovering nicely*)

I knock people out.

ELIZABETH (*Bright*)

My goodness, aren't you quick! Coffee all made?

CAROL

Too many cooks. Where's Fred?

ELIZABETH
(*Hesitates just a split second*)

I can't bring myself to tell you.

CAROL (*Shrugs*)

He can't be far: I'm still here.

OSCAR (HE *smiles, too*)

You hold yourself in high regard.

CAROL (*Matter-of-fact*)

No: accurate regard. I'm not your dumb brunette for nothing.
(*Laughs*)
Do you know I'm a natural blonde? I dye it brunette 'cause
I look cheap as a blonde? I look cheap natural?

ELIZABETH (*Delighted*)

You don't! Are you really!?
(*To the audience*)
Isn't that extraordinary!?

CAROL (*To get* JO's *attention*)

Jo!?

ELIZABETH (*Protective; to* CAROL)

Hsshhh! Don't bother her!

CAROL

JO!?

JO
(*Stirs, looks vaguely about to see who's calling her*)

Hm? What?

CAROL (*Louder*)

JO!?

JO (*Focusing on* CAROL)

What . . . what's happened?

CAROL (*Points at* SAM)

Take a look over there; take a look at Sam.

JO
(*Looks over at* SAM *for quite a long time; turns to*
ELIZABETH; *sort of dreamy*)

Why is . . . why is Sambo all . . . asleep?

ELIZABETH (*Sweet*)

So he'll be nice; he wasn't being nice.

JO
(*Almost interested; sort of sad*)

What happened?

ELIZABETH
(*A look at* CAROL; *to* JO, *a secret*)

He wasn't happy with the way things are. He wanted everything back the way it never was.

JO

That's not nice.

ELIZABETH

No; it isn't.

CAROL (*Eyes to heaven*)

Jesus!

JO (*Sort of lost*)

I don't understand.

ELIZABETH
(*Pulls* JO *to her, head to lap*)

You rest now.

CAROL (*Matter-of-fact*)

Sooner or later you're going to have to wake him up.

ELIZABETH (*Laughs*)

Well, of course!

OSCAR

Certainly you don't imagine we've thought of this as a . . .
final solution.

CAROL (*No nonsense*)

Who *are* you?

ELIZABETH (*Grand*)

I beg your pardon?

CAROL

You can come off it for me; I don't count; I'm an outsider.
Who are you, *really*?

ELIZABETH
(*Observing Carol carefully*)
Oscar, the natural blonde is suspicious.

OSCAR
I noticed.

CAROL
Sam says . . .

ELIZABETH
Sam says! Sam says!

OSCAR
What does Sam know?
(*To the audience*)
What does Sam know? Sam only knows what *Sam* needs.

CAROL
Sam has rights, you know.

OSCAR (*To* CAROL)
And what about what Jo needs? What does what Sam needs
have to do with that?

CAROL (*Dogmatic, if uncertain*)
Things are either true or they're not.

OSCAR
Oh? Really?
(*To the audience*)
Really?
(FRED *enters*)

FRED (To CAROL)

What'd they do: throw you outta the kitchen?

CAROL (*Curiously angered*)

Where the fuck have you been?

FRED

(*Prissy and overarticulating*)

Powdering my nose.

CAROL

Whyn't ya untie Sam?

FRED (*To* OSCAR)

You gonna keep him like this all day? Whyn't you wake him up?

OSCAR

Really?

(*To* ELIZABETH)

Shall I?

ELIZABETH

Try. See what happens.

OSCAR (*Shrugs*)

All right.

(HE *wakes* SAM *up*)

Voilà!

SAM

(*At once; as loud as possible*)

HELP!? HELP!? HELP!? HELP!?

(*Etc., until* OSCAR's *slaps—below—stop him*)

FRED

Jesus!

OSCAR
(*To* FRED)

You see? I told you.

(*To* SAM, *slapping*)
Now! . . . you! . . . stop! . . . that!
(SAM *gasps, sobs a bit, subsides*)

FRED (*Shakes his head*)

Jesus!

SAM

Help me? Someone?

OSCAR

Behave yourself!

SAM (*Softly; in his throat*)

Someone? Help me?

JO (*An echo*)

Help me; help me.

SAM

Carol, can you . . . ?

FRED (*Unpleasant*)
Carol isn't here to *help you*. Keep your hands off him, Carol.

JO (*As above*)

Help me; help me.

SAM

Fred? Please?

CAROL (*To* SAM; *kind*)

Fred isn't here to help you either. I don't think *any*one is.
(LUCINDA *and* EDGAR *reenter*, LUCINDA *leading the
way*; THEY *have trays—cups, plates, coffee, toast,
marmalade, etc.*)

LUCINDA

My gracious, what yelling! What's going *on?!*

EDGAR (*Slightly embarrassed*)

Coffee; coffee, everyone.

LUCINDA

What's going on!!?

SAM (*Softly*)

Help me? Help me, please?

EDGAR (*Puts his tray down*)

Hey, Sam; hey, boy!

SAM

God, Edgar, help me?

LUCINDA (*To the audience*)

What's going *on!?*

EDGAR
(*To* OSCAR; *to* FRED; *to them* ALL)

You gonna untie him now?

OSCAR

We woke him and how did he repay us: he shrieked to raise the very dead.

ELIZABETH (*Softly*)

The very dead; who hear nothing; who remember nothing; who are nothing.

EDGAR

Was that Sam?

LUCINDA
(*Still to the audience; delighted*)

Was that Sam? Was all that yelling Sam?

CAROL

Getting off on it, Lu?

LUCINDA (*To* CAROL)

Pardon?

SAM

Edgar!? Help me!

LUCINDA

Leave Edgar alone; *you* don't love Edgar; you don't love anyone.

EDGAR (*More sad than sarcastic*)

Oh, he loves me, Lu: I'm the only man he knows does something good and he wants to hit; I am his only friend whose every virtue embarrasses him.

SAM

Oh, God, Edgar!

LUCINDA

We don't forget, Sam; we forgive, but we don't forget.

OSCAR (To SAM; *cheerful*)

I like your friends.
(*To the audience*)
I like his friends.

CAROL (*Matter-of-fact*)

I'll untie him; I don't know him; I'm not his friend; I'll untie him.

FRED

Keep your fucking hands off him.

CAROL

'Cause I'm not his friend?

LUCINDA

It's getting cold. Who will have what? I know about you, Edgar.

EDGAR (*Offhand*)

I don't want any.

LUCINDA (*Pours for him*)

Don't be silly.

FRED

I'm a lush, Lu; don't give *me* any coffee.

LUCINDA (*Furious*)

You *asked* for coffee! You yelled at Carol!

FRED
(*Waving* LUCINDA *off; dismissing her*)
I wanted her out of the room; I wanted her to shut up; fuck
your coffee.
(*Afterthought*)
Fuck *you*, for that matter.

LUCINDA (*Defend me!*)
Edgar?

ELIZABETH
(*Half to break into the argument*)
I will have mine with white sugar and real cream; and if that
stuff is instant take it all back into the kitchen and pour it
down the drain.

SAM (*Intense; a supplication*)
The coffee is not instant, the sugar is white and the cream
is real, I have no friends, please let me go.

CAROL
If you're a lush, why should I marry you?

FRED (*Another dismissing wave*)
You'll marry worse. I'm not so bad.

OSCAR
(*To* ELIZABETH *and generally; taking* ELIZABETH *her
coffee and toast*)
"The coffee is not instant, the sugar is white and the cream
is real." Here you are, my dear. "I have no friends, please let
me go." Really!

ELIZABETH
Thank you. You spilled! You sloppy man!

OSCAR (*Indicates* LUCINDA)
She spilled; I wouldn't spill.

LUCINDA (*Enraged*)
I didn't spill! I *never* spill! *You* spilled!

OSCAR (*A calming tone*)
Very *well*; you didn't spill; no one spilled; there has been no
. . . spillage. Spillage?

ELIZABETH (*Shrugs*)
Why not?

SAM
Please? Untie me? Let me go?

LUCINDA
Carol? Cream and sugar?

CAROL
(*Her attention on* SAM, *etc.*)
Nah; I don't want your coffee.

LUCINDA (*A little laugh*)
It is not . . . *my coffee.*

EDGAR (*An edge to his voice*)
No one *wants* it, Lu!

OSCAR (*Dusts his palms*)
I'm going up.
(HE *moves toward the stairway*)

SAM (*Helpless suspicion*)
Where are you going!?

OSCAR

Up.

SAM

Don't *go* up there!

OSCAR

There's no one upstairs. What can you possibly mind?

SAM
(*Enraged by both the constraint and the action*)
DON'T GO UP THERE!!

EDGAR (*Mild; rational*)
Why are you going up there?

OSCAR
(*Considers it as* HE *takes a few more steps up; smiles*)
Because I've never *been*.

SAM (*Trying to break loose*)
YOU HAVE NO RIGHT!!

JO (*Vague*)
Who? Who has no what?

CAROL (*Softly; to* OSCAR)
You *don't* have any right, you know.

OSCAR (*To* ELIZABETH; *laughs*)
Tell them. Tell them all. Give them a reading about rights.
(*Starts up again; to audience*)
Christ, these people!
(HE *disappears into the upstairs hallway*)

CAROL (*Shrugs*)

No right at all.

FRED

What are *you* going to be, a troublemaker?

CAROL (*A gentle dismissal*)

Annnnh, go back to your boozing; don't worry about me; I'll fit in; it'll just take a while.

SAM
(*To himself; head down, shaking it*)

No right; no right at all.

ELIZABETH
(*Putting down her cup; to* SAM; *rational*)

These . . . these rights; these rights people do not have.

SAM (*Slowly meeting her eyes*)

Yes?

LUCINDA (*An aside, to* EDGAR)

Did he really say that to you? That he wanted to hit you?

EDGAR

Shhhhhhh.

ELIZABETH
(*Pleased that* SAM *is meeting her eyes*)

Are these rights rights *no* one has . . . or, merely some?

LUCINDA (*As above*)

What's she talking about?

EDGAR

SHHHHHHH! Jesus!

SAM

Merely some.

ELIZABETH

Aha! Then, there are rights which *you* possess . . .

SAM

In this *house!*

ELIZABETH

. . . which are yours alone!

SAM

In this house!

ELIZABETH (*Smooth*)

Good; then we are not talking about the rights we pretend
we give ourselves in this bewildered land of ours—life, liberty, and the pursuit of the unattainable—though we *may* be
learning our limits—finally—here in the . . . last of the
democracies. Or just about.

LUCINDA (*Offended*)

The *last!*

ELIZABETH

Oh . . . probably; we're too moral to survive. A *real* Nixon
will come along one day, if the Russians don't.

LUCINDA (*Disgusted*)

You're a cynic!

ELIZABETH (*Truly bewildered*)

Am I!? Dear God!

SAM

I have my *own* rights! My own personal rights! Jo! Pay attention to me!

ELIZABETH

Have you? What—this house? Jo? Surely you don't mean property—nothing as crass as that. Is it dignity you have in mind?

(*To the audience*)

I had a dog named Dignity once—or, that was her name when I got her; I changed it; I called her Jane. She's dead.

(*To* SAM)

Is it Jane you have in mind? Is it dignity?

SAM

Jo!? Please!

ELIZABETH

It is *not* Jane you have in mind; it is Jo.

JO (*Vague*)

Me?

ELIZABETH

Back on the farm, when I was growing up, back on the farm in the outskirts of Dubuque . . .

SAM (*So weary*)

You did not grow up on a farm; you did not grow up on the outskirts of—

ELIZABETH

Will you let me finish the story!?

FRED
(*Pointing at him with his glass; not nice*)
Sam, you shut up and let her talk.

SAM
Get out of my house.

EDGAR
Take it easy, Sam.

SAM
Get out of my house! *Both* of you! *All* of you! *All* of you get
out!

JO (*Far away*)
Did you want something, Sam?

ELIZABETH (*Patient*)
Back on the farm, in the outskirts of Dubuque . . .

SAM (*At the top of his lungs*)
OUT?! OUT?! OUT?! OUT?!
(*Etc.*
During this, FRED *puts his drink down, walks over
to* SAM, *punches him hard in the stomach;* SAM *dou-
bles over as best* HE *can; gasps*)

FRED (To SAM)
You don't throw people out of *any*where, you superior bas-
tard. We'll leave when we're finished.
(*Pause; generally*)
I'm finished.
(HE *turns to go; to* CAROL)
You coming?

CAROL (*A sneer*)
Whyn't you wait around and see if you killed him?

EDGAR
Christ, Fred.

FRED
(*Of* SAM; *to* CAROL; *oddly enraged*)
Look at him! *He's* alive! *Look* at him!
(*Indeed,* SAM *is gasping*)

EDGAR
Sam?

FRED
YOU COMING!? I SAID I'M GOING. YOU COMING!?

CAROL (*Pause; calm*)
I think I'll have a cup of coffee before I go. Lucinda, I
think I'll have a cup of coffee after all.
(FRED *moves to the coffee service, sweeps it to the
floor*)

J O (*Faint; at the sound*)
Oh; oh.

FRED
There's no more coffee.
(*Between his teeth*)
You coming?

CAROL
I'll stay for a little; I'll help clean up the mess.

FRED (*Pause; cold*)
I'll wait for you in the car.

CAROL (*Nods*)
O.K. And if you're not there when I come out I'll go on
over to the apartment; and if you're not there . . .
(*Shrugs*)
. . . well, I'll just marry somebody else.

FRED (*Pause; equivocal*)
I'll wait in the car.
(HE *turns; exits.*
A *pause.* LUCINDA *goes to the floor, begins to clean
up*)

EDGAR
(*To* CAROL; *gentle with disbelief*)
You gonna marry that man?

CAROL
(*Looks at him; no emotion*)
You think of any reason why I shouldn't?

EDGAR
(*As* CAROL *moves to help* LUCINDA; *thinks*)
No, no, I guess not.

LUCINDA (*Loss*)
All the pretty cups and saucers.

CAROL (*To* EDGAR)
I didn't think so.
(*To* LUCINDA)
Hey, here's one isn't broken . . . Yes, it is.

EDGAR

You O.K., Sam?

SAM

Sure, Edgar. My wife is dying; I am invaded; I am aban-
doned by my friends. But you really don't care how I am,
Edgar; you didn't raise a finger.

LUCINDA

Don't you have at Edgar that way!

EDGAR (*Quietly raging*)

I *asked* if I could help. Remember? You said no, no one
could help. Remember?

SAM (*Mocking*)

Sure, sure, Edgar.

EDGAR (*Awe and disgust*)

My God, Sam; you don't *want* any help.

SAM

Well, not from you, Edgar; not from you.

EDGAR

(*Rises abruptly, moves to the window seat for his
coat*)
Come on, Lu.

LUCINDA

(*Still with her broken crockery*)
But, Edgar, I'm just . . .

EDGAR

COME ON! If you think I'm going to stay and go through
this!

CAROL
You two going? Did we hit an iceberg?

EDGAR (*Quivering with rage*)
You staying? You wanna watch? O.K. You stay!

CAROL (*Shrugs*)
G'by, rats.

LUCINDA
Don't you talk to Edgar that way!

CAROL (*Moves away from them*)
I was talking to *both* of you.

EDGAR (*To* SAM)
We came over here to *forgive* you!

SAM (*Shakes his head; gently*)
It doesn't matter, Edgar.

EDGAR (*Quivering with rage*)
How *dare* you let this happen to you!

LUCINDA (*Realizing it*)
That's right! We came to forgive you!

SAM (*To stop the exchange*)
It's all right; it doesn't matter.

EDGAR
How *dare* you let this happen! I'm not *here* anymore, Sam.

LUCINDA (*Suddenly in tears*)
I never want to come here again! I never want to come to
this house again!
(*She runs out*)

EDGAR

I'm not *here* anymore, Sam.

SAM (*Pause; accepting*)

O.K., Edgar.

EDGAR
(*Sudden contained emotion*)
I'm not here, God damn you!
(EDGAR *backs into the hall, turns, exits*)

CAROL

Three down and only me to go.

ELIZABETH

Aren't you bright! Why are you marrying that awful man?

CAROL

It's the *least* I can do.

ELIZABETH

You don't have to.

CAROL

I don't? Why don't I? He's on his way downhill; he's a bar-
rel of laughs; he's a lush; he's a great fuck; I'm not doing
anything else this week; I'm not twenty-two anymore, and
I'm scared? Take your choice; they're all true.

ELIZABETH
(*This and the following both to the audience and
generally to* SAM *and* CAROL)
In the outskirts of Dubuque, on the farm, when I was growing up—back there, back then—I learned, with all the pigs
and chickens and the endless sameness everywhere you
looked, or thought, back there I learned—though I doubt I

knew I was learning it—that all of the values were relative
save one . . . "Who am I?" All the rest is semantics—
liberty, dignity, possession.
   (SHE *leans forward; only to* SAM *now*)
There's only one that matters: "Who *am* I?"

        SAM *(Simple)*
I don't *know* who I am.

      ELIZABETH
Then how can you possibly know who I am?
   (OSCAR *appears on the balcony, dressed in* SAM's
   nightshirt, nothing else. HE *poses*)

       OSCAR *(To the* GROUP)
Do I look well? Does it suit me?
   (CAROL *giggles*)

      ELIZABETH
   (*Claps* HER *hands together in delight*)
Oscar! You are a dream!

       JO *(Looks up)*
Sam? Is that you?

       SAM *(Pain)*
Oh, Jo! Don't!

       OSCAR *(To* CAROL)
Don't you think I make a splendid Sam?

       JO
Sam? Is that you?

       SAM
Jo? Please don't?

OSCAR (*Arms wide; beatific*)
Am I not . . . am I, indeed, not Sam?
                    (*To the audience*)
Am I not Sam?

CAROL

I'm going to untie him.

OSCAR

It's on your shoulders, pretty lady; you open the package, you take the present.

CAROL

That's O.K. by me; I'm not a friend.
                    (SHE *unties* SAM)
Who the fuck tied these knots?

OSCAR

Duh menfolk; dey tied him up; dem's duh ones.

SAM

Jo?

JO

Sam?

CAROL

You *wanna* be untied, don't you?

SAM

Sure.

CAROL

It's the least I can do.

SAM

Don't go.

CAROL

Everyone else has gone.

SAM

Yes!

CAROL (*Shrugs*)

What do you want me to do?

SAM (*Lost little boy*)

Make Jo better? Make them go away?
(OSCAR *shakes his head;* ELIZABETH *laughs gently*)

CAROL (*To* SAM; *gentle*)

Jo thinks she's better. They make her think so.

SAM (*Chilling knowledge*)

Is that what matters?

CAROL

Ask Jo.

SAM
(*One final time; but soft, lost*)

Please? That's not Jo's mother?

CAROL
(*After a long pause; totally noncommittal*)

Right. I mean . . . who's to say?
(*To the audience*)

Who's to say?

ELIZABETH
(*Rises, moves toward* CAROL)
You're a very special lady.

CAROL (*A rueful laugh*)
You're pretty special yourself.
(*Looks up at* OSCAR; *ironic*)
You're not so bad, either.
(SHE *looks once more at* SAM; *exits*)

OSCAR (*Waves*)
Bye-bye; bye-bye.

SAM (*Soft*)
Don't go.

JO (*An echo*)
Bye-bye; bye-bye.
(*A silence. Finally,* SAM *rushes from his chair, over
to* JO. ELIZABETH *gestures* OSCAR *not to interrupt.*
SAM *kneels by* JO, *grabs her by the shoulders, shakes
her. We see that* SHE *is rubber.* OSCAR *watches from
his position on the stairs.* ELIZABETH *stays where
SHE was standing with* CAROL)

SAM
(*Tears; choking; loss; fury; tenderness*)
Do you want this? Hunh?
(*Shakes her*)
Is this what you want!? Yes!?

ELIZABETH (*Level; gentle*)
Of course she wants it. Just . . . let her go.

SAM (*Shakes her*)

Because if this is what you want, I'm not any part of it;
you've locked me out. I . . . I don't exist. I . . . I don't
exist. Just . . . just *tell* me.

(JO *manages to look at him, puts her hands to his
face, cups it*)

JO (*Explaining; gently*)

Please . . . just let me die?

(SAM *pulls away, stares at her, wracked with sobs.
To the audience; explaining*)

Just let me die . . . please?

(*Here her explanation begins to become pain*)

PLEASE? . . .

(*This time the word is prolonged as long as possible; it is urged out by pain; it is filled with gasps;
to no one, to everyone. Now* SHE *grasps her belly
in short spasms of pain*)

Anhhh! Anhhh! ANHHHHH!

(OSCAR *comes down the stairs to her*)

OSCAR

All right; all right, now.

(SAM *watches the following without moving from
his position; his sobs continue, though*)

JO

Aaaaaaaaaaaannnnnnnhhhh! Sweet Jesus! Aaaaaaaaaannnnn-
nnhhhhhhhh!

OSCAR

(*Scooping her into his arms*)

Let me help you.

SAM

Jo!

JO
(*Through her gasps; to* OSCAR)
Just . . . get . . . me . . . up . . . stairs.

SAM
Jo?

OSCAR
(*As* HE *carries her upstairs; soothing, crooning*)
I'll take care of you now; I'll make you better; you'll see; I'll
put you right to bed; I'll make you better . . .

JO
Just get me . . . AAAANNNNHHHHHHH!

OSCAR
(*As* HE *carries her Offstage*)
Shhhh, shhhh, shhhh; easy, now; easy.
(*A howl from Offstage; another*)

ELIZABETH
(*Moves to a chair; gently*)
She's dying, you see.

SAM (*Sobs under; shivering*)
I'*m* dying.

ELIZABETH
Oh, no; not yet. You don't know what it *is*.
(*A softer howl from upstairs;* ELIZABETH *laughs
abruptly; then smiles*)
I had a dream once about dying. Shall I tell it to you?

SAM (*Shivering*)
No.

ELIZABETH

All right: I dreamt I was on a beach at sunset—with friends;
we had a driftwood fire, I believe.

SAM

I don't want to know.

ELIZABETH
(*Begins to share this with the audience, too*)
There were seagulls in the distance, and there was the sound
of the surf—but muted, for it was sunset.

SAM

I don't want to know.

ELIZABETH

And all at once . . . it became incredibly quiet; the waves
stopped, and the gulls hung there in the air.

SAM

No? Please?

ELIZABETH

Such silence. And then it began; the eastern horizon was
lighted by an explosion, hundreds of miles away—no sound!
And then another, to the west—no sound! And within sec-
onds they were everywhere, always at a great distance—the
flash of light, and silence.

SAM

Please?

ELIZABETH

We knew what we were watching, and there was no time to
be afraid. The silence was . . . beautiful as the silent bombs

went off. Perhaps we were already dead; perhaps that was
why there was no sound.
> (*A silence*)

SAM (*A shivering little boy*)
That was . . . that was the end of the world.

ELIZABETH
> (*A pause; comforting; to* SAM, *now*)
I thought that's what we were talking about.
> (*To the audience*)
Isn't that what we were talking about?
>> (OSCAR *appears in the upstairs hallway, dressed in
>> his own clothes.*
>> *To* OSCAR)
Is it all right?

OSCAR (*Looks down at them*)
Yes; it's all right.
> (*Indicates*)
And that one?

ELIZABETH
He's better; calmer.

SAM (*Still the little boy*)
It *is* true, isn't it? What you told me?

ELIZABETH (*Dreamy*)
No sound? No time to be afraid? Everything done before
you know it?

SAM
Yes. It is true?

ELIZABETH

Everything is true.

OSCAR
(*Descending. Quietly; to* ELIZABETH; *to* SAM)
Therefore, nothing is true.

ELIZABETH (*Looks up at him*)
Therefore, everything is true.
(SHE *smiles*)

OSCAR
(*Descending.* HE *smiles; an endearment*)
Oh, Elizabeth.
(*A silence*)

SAM

And Jo?

ELIZABETH (*Tiny pause*)
Don't worry about Jo.

OSCAR

We can go now.

ELIZABETH
(*Vaguely, momentarily surprised*)
What? Yes, of course we can.
(SHE *stands*)

SAM

No time to be afraid?

ELIZABETH

No! No time!

SAM (*More insistent*)

No time to be afraid!?

ELIZABETH

No! No time! Everything done before you know it.

SAM

. . . Before I know it.

ELIZABETH

Everything done.

OSCAR
(*Faintly contemptuous, to the audience*)

Nothing is retained; nothing. Come.

ELIZABETH

All right.

SAM
(*Finally; timid; to* ELIZABETH)

Who are you? Really?

ELIZABETH
(*Looks at him for a moment*)

Why, I'm the lady from Dubuque. I thought you knew.
(*To the audience*)

I thought he knew.

CURTAIN

EDWARD ALBEE

Edward Albee was born March 12, 1928, and began writing plays thirty years later. His plays are,
in order of composition: *The Zoo Story*; *The
Death of Bessie Smith*; *The Sandbox*; *The American Dream*; *Who's Afraid of Virginia Woolf?*;
The Ballad of the Sad Cafe (adapted from Car-
son McCuller's novella); *Tiny Alice*; *Malcolm*
(adapted from James Purdy's novel); *A Delicate
Balance*; *Everything in the Garden* (adapted from
a play by Giles Cooper); *Box and Quotations
from Chairman Mao Tse-Tung*; *All Over*; *Sea-
scape*; *Listening*; *Counting the Ways* and *The
Lady From Dubuque*.